This book is dedicated to all my past selves and my wife Sully.

RESET YOUR MINDSET

How to get your sh*t together by befriending your brain and your body

Jenn Baron

Canoe Tree
Press

4697 Main Street
Manchester Center, VT 05255
Canoe Tree Press is a division of DartFrog Books

Table of Contents

Introduction

Hi there, I'm Jenn, thank you for checking out my book. I'm really glad you're here! Picture a Labrador Retriever whose butt is gonna wiggle right off! That's how glad I am!

I wrote this book because there are things that, once I learned, I wanted everyone else to know because they blew my mind. Things that made me realize, "Maybe I'm not broken, messed up, and alone in how I think and feel." That was huge and life-changing for me because those adjectives describe how I felt the first 40-ish years of my life.

I've included straight forward, in layman's terms, things about our brains and bodies that have helped me get unstuck, *genuinely* like myself for more than a stretch of a couple hours, or days, and not in a cheesy affirmation-y way, and feel like I have my spark back that I've let dulled over the years. And I'm not a unicorn (well I am unique and so are you) but everything in this book 100% applies to you, no exceptions! Not one, I pinky promise. I'll show you exactly why throughout the book.

The following stories are from my own life, the lives of my life coaching clients, and close humans. You might not have had the exact same experiences, but I know you'll be able to take something from each story and apply it to your life. The details of what we experience are different, but we're all doing our best to navigate the stuff that comes with being human. The good, the not so good, and everything in between. We all have times when we feel not good enough, alone, broken, hopeless, and like a victim.

I like straight forward and user-friendly in all things.

I like Cheetos, belting out 80's music, my wife Sully's smash burgers we have most Friday nights, watching all the Hallmark

Christmas movies with our black Labs, Georgia and Carolina, the first sip of hazelnut coffee with sugar-free French vanilla creamer, my electric mattress pad in the winter (that was a genius invention!), and pepperoni, mushroom, and extra cheese pizza is my fave food on the planet. Preferably with a thick crust and a caffeine-free diet Pepsi.

I like information to be "easily digestible" and not "tough and chewy" accompanied with a "what the hell" look on my face when I'm trying to understand it.

Clutter makes me bonkers and slows down my brain, the ocean and mountains are my happy places, I don't think we use swear words often enough, having fun is completely underrated for adults, "Zootopia" is my favorite movie, followed by "Despicable Me," Sully is a phenomenal cook (thank God because I don't enjoy it at all), she's my biggest cheerleader and best friend (even when I'm being very human, emotionally messy, and don't want to talk about what's really going on in my brain).

I prefer things that don't take much effort and give me lots of rewards.

I was diagnosed with Generalized Anxiety Disorder almost 20 years ago, which I now see completely differently and dismiss that label. I love to jump on trampolines even though I always feel like I'm going to pee my pants a little and often do. I have to have Count Chocula every Halloween season, I admire the hell out of resourcefulness, slow drivers and shoppers make me ragey, I name all my cars, breakfast for dinner is fun. I have 13 tattoos, I used to wake up every morning with loads of anxiety, I love to organize and purge stuff, and my mom and sister passed from Huntington's Disease (for which I tested negative, thank God).

The stories in this book will help raise your awareness of what's going on in your normal and amazing brain and body. We can't change what we don't see and acknowledge.

These stories will help you realize and accept that you are not broken or alone in your thoughts and feelings. Each and every one of us thinks we're the exception to this but we aren't. We are basically the same with slightly different shades and nuances that make us fantastically individual.

And because I like practical, do-almost-anywhere solutions, I've included oodles of my favorite practices that will help you better understand, and start to befriend, your brain and body so you can repair your relationship with yourself.

I used to wake up every morning with feelings of anxiety followed by a chunk of time spent answering the unhelpful question of, "What's wrong with me?" Spoiler alert, the answer for all of us is, nothing, and I'll tell you why.

This book is a lot like a coaching session with me. It's not linear because life *isn't* linear.

Some chapters will teach you something about yourself to give you greater awareness of what's going on in your brain and body and the simple explanation as to why. We can't tweak what we don't see.

Other chapters will help you see that our brains operate the same way and are only trying to protect us and keep us alive (thanks brain).

And some chapters include my favorite easy-to-do practices that will help you stop living your life from the neck up. There's so much untapped wisdom and guidance in our bodies, so let's take kitten steps to glean what is our birthright.

In addition to being a coach, I also practice massage therapy and bodywork. Working with people in this way and creating a safe and comfortable space for them to be quiet and let go a little, is something I will always hold close to my heart. And it's where I first saw the strong connection between how our bodies hold onto unprocessed emotions. That knot in your neck or near your shoulder blade? Might be something you're holding onto. I'm pretty woo-woo but also love me some science-based evidence! There's room for all of it.

You don't need to be fixed, because you're not broken. This book will help you see that, get unstuck, and get moving in the direction you really want to go.

I'm cheering so hard for you!

You got this, Sunshine, and I've got your back!

CHAPTER 1

How Our Brains Work

A good foundation is important whether you're talking about a house, relationship, or math. We can't do algebra problems without learning how to add and subtract. Learning about the following parts of our brains and how they dictate what we do, helped me finally believe I wasn't broken, messed up, or doomed to keep making the same mistakes. This will be interesting, useful, and give you a foundation for the rest of what we'll cover.

The following definitions and examples are going to open your eyes to why change is always possible and how your brain is normal and healthy like everyone else's. Let's dive in.

Neuroplasticity is the scientific name and explanation as to why we can change. It describes how the brain is designed. There's a phrase, "What fires together, wires together," and refers to our nerve cells called neurons. They're pathways in our brains that wire together with lots of repetition. This means that repetition creates our lives, for better or worse.

When we think or do something over and over, it creates a superhighway in our brain that becomes automatic. You probably have a routine when you take a shower. I wash my hair, then face, then body. I rarely change them around. I could alter my order of showering and then I would create a different automatic neural super-highway.

Neuroplasticity enables our thoughts and habits to grow and change. The beautiful thing is that we can always rewire our neural pathways; it just takes repetition. Even if you've thought the same crappy thought for decades, or have a behavior that doesn't serve you, you can change it and it won't take decades. Awesome news, right?!

The limbic system (alarm/primitive brain) is the oldest and most primitive part of our brain. It's only concerned with keeping you alive so you can potentially keep the species going. It's the fight-flight-freeze part of our brain, so when our brain perceives anything as a threat, it activates the limbic system.

Over our 650 million years on this planet, our brains have learned that three things keep you alive. Decreasing your pain, increasing your pleasure, and do everything as efficiently as possible.

Brains have learned that if you're experiencing pain, your life could be in danger. This goes for physical and emotional pain because they follow a similar path in the brain when they're being perceived. That's why we resist feelings and emotions we see as painful. Our brains think they could kill us, so they want us to avoid them.

Brains have also learned that when you're experiencing pleasure, that usually leads to continued survival, so it wants you to watch more TV, eat more cookies, play, and have more fun.

Lastly, brains *love* efficiency and conserving energy. They want you to have as much energy as possible in case you have to outrun a tiger. Imagine if we had to relearn how to turn a doorknob each time we walked up to a door. Our species would never survive. Brains learn, they learn fast, and automate as much as possible. Fun tidbit: of all our organs, our brains burn the most calories. When I first learned that I thought, "Well I should be skinny as a rail then for all the worrying and thinking I've done!"

This is one reason that new habits are challenging. Our brains want us to stick to what's easy and familiar instead of taking the time and energy to learn new things because you could need that energy for said tiger. This is also the reason we can easily revert back to old behavior. Our brains don't want you to use energy to do the new thing, so it'll try to convince you not to. It's up to us to be aware of its shenanigans and go in the direction we want.

Knowing these three things about our primitive brains explains so much, if not all of human behavior. Everything falls into one or more of these categories. Your brain is just trying to keep you alive. Sometimes we need to tweak what we're thinking and doing because they don't serve us anymore. But now we can turn down the volume on shame and blame because it's just our sweet, normal human brains trying to keep us alive. Thanks to neuroplasticity, we can change what doesn't serve us pretty quickly!

The prefrontal cortex is involved in higher cognitive functions including memory, attention, planning, creativity, and problem solving. This is the part of the brain that we want to operate from as often as possible. This is the "adult" part of our brain, and the limbic system is the "toddler" part. It's never a good thing to let the toddler run the show. Another important tidbit, the primitive brain and the prefrontal cortex cannot be "online" at the same time. You're always operating from one or the other, not both.

When we're thinking and behaving from the primitive part of our brains, it's all about survival. Today, we don't have tigers and bears lurking. Instead, it's trying to get the kids to bed without a fight and loads of emails that activate our nervous systems.

Knowing that our limbic system just wants to keep us alive no matter what, we'll use the prefrontal cortex to work *with* our brains, rather than being ruled by our survival-focused and often unhelpful thoughts and actions that don't serve us.

Our brains are so amazing and with just a bit of foundational understanding, you can change the trajectory of your life!

Let's go!

CHAPTER 2

Our Thoughts Aren't True

Our thoughts seem logical, true and accurate, so we rarely question them. Our brains are thinking them so why wouldn't they be correct? They're "coming from inside the house," so they have to be factual. Right?

But the truth is that most of our thoughts are crap. We pick them up through how we were raised, socialized, and by what we came to believe about ourselves and the world. We keep thinking about them for decades because they're habits, and then they become our beliefs. Aren't our thoughts like certified letters from the Universe?

Nope, thoughts are just sentences in your brain. Or what Dr. Russell Kennedy calls brain droppings. I really think this nickname nails it.

They're like the ticker at the bottom of the TV when there's a weather advisory or school closings. We have about 60,000 thoughts a day. Kinda bananas right?! About 95% of them are subconscious and fly under our radar. Some of these thoughts are the negative ones on repeat that we accept as facts. Like it is what it is and we're reporting the weather out our windows.

We don't question them, try to poke holes in them, or "look under their hood." I'd bet all the pizza in the world–that's the biggest bet I could make because I love me some pizza–that your thoughts are ruling, and possibly ruining, your life.

Your thoughts and feelings are on a loop, and the loop dictates your actions; your actions lead to your results. Part of the formula for living your favorite life is to examine and tweak the thoughts and feelings that aren't serving you. This helps you see you can be in control of your life. We're not in control of all the circumstances in life, but we always get to decide how to think, feel, and respond to a situation.

That doesn't mean we throw glitter, rainbows, and daisies on everything, AKA toxic positivity, or sweep things under the rug. Nope, we don't do that around here. Been there, done that, and it always felt like shit. Just with glitter everywhere making a big mess.

You get to *decide* how you want to show up in each situation.

That feels more powerful, doesn't it?

Feels less victim-y, doesn't it?

Start by watching your thoughts. Especially the 'frequent fliers,' and ones you believe as absolute truth.

Thoughts like:

- I can't say no when someone asks me to do something.
- I guess I'm always going to have issues with food.
- I've tried to change but it never works.
- I could never start a podcast, have a hard conversation with my spouse, or find a new job.
- Life will be better when I lose weight, my kids are out of the house, or I get my next certification.
- I'm not good enough.

What thought/feeling loops are keeping you stuck? I bet you can name a few off the top of your head. What thoughts feel true? Like really, really true? Like you're just stating the weather outside. Let's take a look at what these untrue thoughts could look like and then examine how we could change them.

- I am someone who isn't taken seriously at work.
- I am not talented enough to be a full-time artist (or a musician, or a writer, or someone who flips houses).
- I can't leave this relationship because this is the best I can do.

Instead, would you like to be:

- Someone who stands up for themselves?
- Someone who pursued their passion and turned into a livelihood?
- Someone who doesn't settle?
- Someone who deserves healthy love and companionship?

All you need is a tiny crack in your old thought and to process its feeling energy. That crack is where the light and healing will enter.

CHAPTER 3

Kitten Steps

At one time or another we've all been told to take baby steps. To slow your roll so you can get your wobbly feet steady before you try to walk or run. I get it and I love a good analogy. But I've heard another that resonates with me more, so I have to share it with you.

Victoria Albina, one of my fantastic life coaches, first used the term kitten steps to describe this idea. It gave me all the warm and fuzzy feels, so I decided to adopt the term immediately. The idea of a tiny 8-week-old kitten gingerly making their way around your home for the first time is so precious to me and that's how I want to see myself more and more.

When you bring a kitten home, it's best to secure them in a small room so they can feel a sense of safety in their new surroundings. You don't just let them roam free in the whole house; it's too much, especially if there are other pets or kids around. That would totally overwhelm their tiny nervous systems and freak them out.

The same thing happens to our nervous systems when we try to change a bunch of things all at once, we get a diagnosis, or get the dreaded 2am phone call. Our nervous systems don't have the capacity to hold or absorb it all at once and we often go into fight/flight/freeze mode while we try to wrap our brains and hearts around the information.

I'm not into freaking out our little kitten-like nervous systems around here. I'm about doable, approachable, manageable steps and changes. Your primitive brain is instantly going to tell you that kitten steps aren't enough, because it doesn't want you to change. It wants you to stay in the illusion of safety by *not* making any changes. It'll tell you lies like:

- Don't bother walking for 20 minutes because that's not enough to help you lose weight.
- Don't apply for the job promotion because you know Karen in accounting will try to undermine you anyway.
- Don't set that boundary with your MIL because it'll rock the whole boat, even though you're so tired of her making comments about your parenting, clothing, or food choices.
- Just keep doing all the things at home and work because it's "easier" and no one will help.

Those mean comments are your brain's way of trying to keep you safe. When my brain is doing this, I'll say something like, "Thank you sweet melon, I appreciate you looking out for me, and I'm going to take the kitten step because it's what we want/need and we will be glad we did even if it's not right this second." I talk to my brain a lot. Like a lot, a lot. Our brains can be like an annoying backseat driver constantly telling you to go a different route; and you can say, "Thanks, I hear you, and I'm going to keep going this way."

By acknowledging your brain's alarm message, it realizes you heard it, and it doesn't have to keep yelling so loudly or as often. Like when a toddler is acknowledged after saying, "Mom!" a thousand times. They usually quiet down because they feel heard. Your primitive brain is like a toddler.

We've been abusive enough to ourselves. We threw ourselves into the deep end of the pool before we could swim very well. Where has it gotten us? Beaten up, bruised, and not trusting ourselves. I invite you to try another way. Try doing things just a bit differently. Taking a tiny kitten step will give your nervous system time to realize it's safe, your ability to do the thing will grow, and so will your confidence.

Little kitten steps are the real way you will make big lasting changes in your life. They set you up for success instead of repeated failure and constantly feeling like crap about yourself. I know you will get to where you want to go when you're kinder to yourself and practice kitten steps.

CHAPTER 4

Our Brains Are Wired to Keep Us Safe

When I decided to write a book, I crowdsourced the smart peeps on social media asking for connections to a developmental and copy editor and got a number of wonderful leads.

And then my brain freaked out because it's normal and healthy. It said stuff like, "Wait, we're really doing this? You're not an author! An editor is going to read a chapter and tell you not to quit your day job. They're going to put a crap ton of 'red marks' all over it because it's not very good."

Our brains can be total assholes sometimes, but they do this to protect us. The primitive part of my brain has no reference for writing a book, so it doesn't know if it's safe. And if it doesn't know if it's safe then it does not want me to do it. It's *very* skeptical of new things and this is all new! It has no clue about the upcoming major learning curves, discomfort, vulnerability, trying, stumbling, face planting, getting up, and trying again.

It wants me to save my energy for important things like fighting off tigers and bears because the primitive part of our brain still thinks that's a possibility. You're seeing 650 million years of evolution in real time. The primitive part wants me to keep doing what I've done, not write a book, and not try new things because it thinks that equals safety and a continuation of my life.

That's how the primitive part of our brains work, and when we start to see that we can work with it, instead of thinking something is wrong, or that it's a "sign" that we shouldn't do the thing. This part is where we can unintentionally cut ourselves off at the knees if we don't know what's really going on in our brains.

But I knew I had a book in me that had to be written. Not writing it was *not* an option. If I didn't write it, it would have been a huge regret on my deathbed, and I wasn't going to do that to myself or to the people that the book would hopefully help one day.

I had a come-to-Jesus talk with myself and made a very conscious decision that the best way through this, and the best way to not give up, was to *plan for the freak outs* and practice what I preach. When I plan that something is going to be challenging or uncomfortable, it makes the challenges a lot easier for me because I'm not expecting all rainbows and butterflies. I'm not making it more difficult, just being realistic and setting myself up for success instead of suffering.

When I'd get an edit back from Meghan, my fantastic developmental editor, and my brain would throw a hissy fit and act like I'll never be able to figure out what to say, then I would kindly talk to my brain and say, "Yep we're doing something new, we haven't done this exact piece before, so of course you're going to freak out, it's ok, that's normal, and it's all a part of this process."

I plan for and anticipate my brain's reaction and see it as part of the process of doing something new that my primitive brain doesn't have a frame of reference for. My brain is trying to protect me from something it thinks is scary, so it sends me a feeling of anxiety to try to derail me. I accept it, don't make a big deal out of it, and keep plugging away at my edits.

What I do now is *plan* for the anxious freaked out feeling. Remind myself that it's normal and expect it. When I expect it, it doesn't catch me off guard or send me down a spiral of doom, and I don't spend much time and energy wishing it away or trying to fix it.

Then I do somatic practices and have conversations with my brain to calm the alarm and remind it we're on the same side. It goes like this, "Hi sweet brain, thank you for the warning, I appreciate you. I know we're doing something new and kinda scary and it's your job to keep me safe and alive, thank you. We've got this, I'm taking it slow, stretching our nervous system but not snapping it. It's safe to have fun with this. Let's go, I've got you!"

This awareness and practice have been a game-changer for me. It's helped me start a coaching practice, podcast, have tough conversations with my wife and in business, and teach workshops.

Your brain is doing exactly what it's supposed to when it sends you alarm messages. And when you know what's going on, and how to work with them, you don't have to let them get in the way of going for the things you want.

Notice the messages and keep going for it!

CHAPTER 5

Productive Struggle

I've had four dogs as an adult. Two sets of female Lab litter-mates. Gus (a yellow) and Coco (a chocolate) and then Georgia and Carolina (both black).

Our first pair didn't start out as a pair, but Sully hoodwinked me into it, and I'm so grateful.

We went back and forth between a few different breeds, but my dad always had Labs as hunting dogs. I grew up with them, they were my confidants and true BFFs, I loved them so hard, and I'm grateful my wife agreed to go with that option. And they're adorable puppies! So easy to say yes to their soft ears and pudgy tummies!

We went to get Gus (named after Sully who woke up one morning at age 10, only wanting to be called Gus) in Ohio, and when we arrived and knocked on the door, we could see through the glass that there was a yellow puppy chasing its mom, and we just had a feeling that she was ours. We were right, and what we could see through the glass was a small glimpse of the fun that was in store for us.

As we were talking to the breeders, getting papers signed, and giving them our money, Sully asked if there were any puppies not spoken for. The woman said yes, there were a couple chocolate pups and would we like to see them? I knew I was screwed; I gave my wife the side eye, and told her to hold off on filling out the check. I went to where the other pups were, picked one up, and she snuggled into my neck. I was a goner. This was Coco and she came home with us too. Sully is an evil genius and I'm so glad.

While getting two puppies had its challenges, it was the best decision for our family, and we loved that they had each other. They were BFFs from the start, but we did make one big mistake, in that we didn't create "separate time" so they could get comfortable being without each other. And when we had to say goodbye to Coco 11 years later, it was really hard on Gus.

Fast forward to now-ish, and we have Carolina and Georgia, they're four years old. Georgia's tummy wasn't feeling well, and our vet could see her for a drop-off appointment. Usually, we'd take Carolina along so they wouldn't be separated. See how we were creating the same problem and separation anxiety? Sully saw what was starting, and suggested Carolina stay with me since I'd be working from home.

My alarm/primitive brain freaked out at first and it sounded like this:

- Are they going to be anxious?
- How's it gonna go?
- Will Georgia be ok at the vet by herself?
- Will Carolina freak the fuck out?
- How am I going to feel managing all these anxious thoughts?

My brain freaks out the most when it comes to my furry kids. I never want anything to be wrong with them or for them to feel any discomfort because then I have uncomfortable feels. This is an area where I'm very much a work in progress.

I decided some discomfort on my part was worth it in the long run because we want them to feel comfortable being by themselves and didn't want them to have the same separation anxiety that Gus and Coco felt during their lives and after we lost Coco.

I explained to Georgia and Carolina what the day was going to look like. They seemed semi cool with it. And I explained to my alarm/primitive brain that, "We're doing something new, and it will be for everyone's good. It's normal to freak out a little and it'll be just fine in the end." I talk to my alarm/brain a lot. Like, a lot, a lot. It's important to tend to our body's alarm, not let our thoughts run the show, and to poke holes at what seems like the "truth," but usually isn't.

The day ended up being such a win. The vet didn't find anything wrong with Georgia, yay; she was fine by herself. And Carolina and I had so much fun together. We went on a walk because we're practicing leash training. She got some apple chunks when I was having my favorite snack, a Honeycrisp apple and peanut butter. She was my assistant during a coaching call, although she slept through it, slacker. And overall, she did so well!

Like Sully says, it was productive struggle. The experience stretched us all in helpful ways and we're all better for it. I was willing to be uncomfortable because I knew it was the best thing for everyone.

I'm grateful Sully made the suggestion and I'm so proud of us for doing it! We did something challenging and a little freaky-outty, but now it'll be easier the next time they need to be separated for some reason. This experience also gave my alarm/primitive brain proof and evidence that we can stretch our comfort zone and we won't die. Remember, our alarm/primitive brain's only concern is our safety and keeping us alive. It thought we might die from separating them and I proved to it that we won't. I tended to the alarm in my body, kept being present with it which allowed it to come and go instead of resisting it like I would in the past.

This practice tends to our alarm, increases our capacity to do hard things, and is how we grow our confidence and self-trust.

The way I coach myself and my clients doesn't involve trying to get rid of life's hard moments or the feelings and thoughts that come along with them. I used to think that was the goal of "self-help-y" stuff and the point of life: to feel awesome as often as possible and get through the shitty parts as fast as possible.

But now I believe it's about having the capacity to manage and maneuver through them. Life will always be 50% yay and 50% boo, and it's how we show up for ourselves, and move through situations that matters. Not about eliminating the hard ones.

You don't have to get rid of struggle or discomfort. They're a normal part of life and not going anywhere. They don't need to. But what I want for myself and you is to say and eventually believe, "In some way, shape, and form, I will be able to handle what comes my way. I will dig deep, maybe I'll ask for help, and I will handle the thing with 1% more kindness and compassion toward myself."

In my opinion, that's winning at life!

CHAPTER 6

Emotional and Physical Pain

Sully and I really enjoy watching the TV series *Master Chef*. She's a *great* cook and gets all sorts of inspiration and thinks about how she'd complete the challenges. I just think about eating the food, LOL.

One of the episodes in season 19 hit me like a ton of bricks. A contestant, Shanika, made a dish she used to make with her mom, who passed away when Shanika was six years old. As Shanika talked about the dish, she was very emotional, and said many times, "I don't like to make this meal because it makes me sad, and I hate feeling sad, or any emotions."

You could see in her body language that she was literally fighting and holding back the emotions. And I get that she'd rather not ugly cry on national TV; stay with me, because I bet you can relate.

Her fierce desire to push down and ignore her emotions in her day-to-day life struck me. She's avoiding normal emotions and pushing them down because she doesn't like how she feels when they come up.

I 100% get that. I really do. I used to be an Olympic level feelings-pusher-downer. I used to rarely acknowledge when I was bothered, upset, annoyed, pissed, or angry. That's not how a "nice" or "good" girl acted. I didn't speak up; I said I was fine when I was the very opposite of fine.

I would eat and drink my feelings, deny them, keep my mouth shut, and pray to all things good and holy that they'd just go the fuck away.

Denial and pushing them away works right?

Nope, sure doesn't.

I'd love to know how avoiding and pushing feelings down is affecting Shanika's daily life. She might experience headaches or migraines, digestive issues, depression, anxiety, irritability, and may have a hard time being comfortable in relationships.

Her primitive brain has been telling her it's too painful to feel the emotions and she might die if she does. Like all human brains, when she feels emotional pain the same areas of the brain are activated as when she feels physical pain. Thanks to evolution and the fact that our brains and bodies always want to be efficient, the same area of the brain is activated when we feel emotional pain as when we feel physical pain. That's why it can literally hurt physically when we lose someone or something we love. This is normal and nothing has gone wrong. When we're aware of what's going on, we have the opportunity to accept it and move through it.

Because our brains process emotional and physical pain in the same area, emotional pain can feel just as dangerous to our survival as physical pain. It's natural to want to avoid pain, but avoiding emotional pain doesn't serve us in the long run and creates ten times the suffering as working through our feelings ASAP.

Shanika is basically creating a suffering sandwich. She's got the suffering of losing her mom, but then she's got the extra layer of denying it and pushing it down and away. If Shanika was a coaching client, and she was ready to do something a little differently, I'd encourage her to do some somatic exercises and compassionately talk back to her brain when it wants her to avoid her feelings.

Something like, "It's possible to feel sad for five seconds and it won't kill me." When she does that, she's creating proof that she won't die. This is what rewiring your brain looks like, and it's how you make a change. It's not complicated and just takes practice.

My goal in life is not to stop feeling anxiety, sadness, or disappointment, but it sure as hell used to be! Today my goal is to accept that all feelings and emotions are ok, and to know that I will handle them with compassion and kindness towards myself. I practice going through it, instead of around it.

CHAPTER 7

Ground Yourself in the Present

We live most of our lives from the neck up. Many of us retreated to our minds because it wasn't safe in our bodies or homes, which were extensions of our bodies. We forget there's so much wisdom, peace, and comfort to be found in our bodies when we come back to them. When we are in our bodies, it's a sign to our alarm/primitive brain, that we are safe, which lowers stress, panic attacks, and helps bring you back to a calmer state.

I love the simplicity of somatic practices; you can do this one anywhere and no one will know what you're doing. I've legit done this in a bathroom stall, in the car, in meetings, during dinner parties, and before presentations.

Start by taking three deep breaths all the way down to your toes. This calms your alarm that's giving you a warning signal. If you're doing this with a kiddo, tell them to pretend they're smelling their favorite flower (for the inhale) and blowing out a candle (for the exhale).

If you're able to say the following out loud, go for it. If not, no worries, just say them to yourself:

- Name five items in your space
- List four colors you see
- Touch three things near you (I'll use my body if I'm in a public bathroom)
- Notice two things you can hear
- And one thing you can smell (hopefully the answer isn't poop, but whatever)

Take three more deep breaths. You can interchange these because there's no wrong way to do it.

This is a fantastic tool for you or your kiddo when they're experiencing a big overwhelming feeling. Somatic practices can be done at almost any age. I think they're some of the best gifts you can give yourself and those around you because it feels like shit to be uncomfortable in your skin or feel out of control in your body. These will help with both challenges.

CHAPTER 8

What Happened When I Went Off Zoloft

In 2018, I noticed my boobs were leaking, and I *absolutely* wasn't pregnant. My first thought was, "oh fuck, is this a sign of breast cancer?"

I went to see my doctor and he said it could be from taking Zoloft, which I've taken since 2005, or a benign tumor on my pituitary gland causing my prolactin levels to be high and therefore, leaky boobs. I freaked out because all I heard was, "Tumor in my head," and to me that meant a brain tumor.

He didn't want me to undergo an unnecessary MRI, so he had me taper off Zoloft very slowly and stay off it for 30 days to see if that changed my prolactin levels.

Spoiler alert: I should've done the MRI!

Under his direction, I slowly (50 mg at a time) came off it and stayed off it for a month. It was about two-and-a-half months from being on my then normal dose, to being completely off it. As I was coming off it, I noticed I was a little dizzy and bumped into things like I'd had too much wine. I also noticed I was a lot more weepy and would cry at most commercials, especially the "sad" ones. I was feeling more feelings, and on deeper levels, than I had in a long time.

I popped into Steak 'n Shake for lunch one day and watched as the two servers busted their asses taking care of the entire restaurant. I was especially moved, actually crying, by how hard one server was working and probably getting crap tips; so I gave her a $20 on my way out and told her that I could see and appreciate her hustle. That experience stuck out because it wasn't "like me" to be that emotional. At Steak 'n' Shake. Over some really hard work.

I used to think taking Zoloft was "cheating" somehow. Like I wasn't trying "natural things" hard enough and that my body had somehow let me down and was defective. I felt defeated. But without Zoloft in my system, it felt like my emotions were spilling out everywhere, on full blast, and I was wearing them all over my sleeves. I felt raw, exposed, and like I didn't have the right tools for the experience.

Sully kept checking in with me to see how I was doing as my medication decreased. She could tell life was getting harder for me to manage. She's a self-proclaimed "weeper," tearing up over lots of things, but I'm not really.

After weaning off Zoloft, nothing changed boob-wise, so I scheduled an MRI which found the tiny benign pituitary tumor.

When I saw my doctor for the follow-up appointment to discuss treating the little bugger, I burst into tears because I was struggling to function. I didn't have the tools to manage all the feelings the medication had been keeping at bay.

We immediately set up a plan to go back on Zoloft and I was so relieved. While getting back on the medication, it was messing with my stomach, and I was having a hard time eating which is never a problem for me. I could never understand how some folks say they forgot to eat. What?! Not this girl. But I'd have a few bites and I'd get this knot in my solar plexus area, just below where your ribs come together in the center of your body. Sully made my favorite meals, but I couldn't get past three or four bites. This freaked us both out because it was so unlike me.

What I know now is that my body's internal background alarm was going off. When that happens, our bodies shut down our digestion in case we need to run or fight off a tiger. My alarm has been going off for decades. I called it anxiety and resigned myself to believing I was broken, and it was just a part of who I am. I just needed to accept this shitty life sentence and get on with it.

Because I couldn't eat much, I was losing weight which I was honestly thrilled about, but knew it wasn't healthy for me because of what was going on in the big picture. We'd heard many times that smoking pot can improve your appetite when you don't feel well so I thought I'd give it a shot.

I was making mac-n-cheese for dinner and while the noodles were boiling, I took a couple hits which sent my body's background alarm off like a smoke detector when my wife cooks bacon. I couldn't get my heart rate to come down, my chest was going from cold to hot to cold, I couldn't take a deep breath, and I felt like I was going to die. I was having my first of many panic attacks. I didn't have the internal resources to calm and soothe myself yet, and I was spinning in and out of different intensities of anxiety and panic.

That evening was the scariest I'd ever experienced. I didn't end up eating dinner and went to bed to try to rest and sleep it off. That didn't happen. I tossed and turned and even heard a male, dark, evil voice tell me to jump out my second-story window. I've never had suicidal thoughts and immediately told Sully, my doctor, and therapist about the voice. I'm grateful it was a one-time thing and that I had the wherewithal to understand what was going on and talk about it.

I was experiencing a primal sense of not being safe, not being able to do anything to control my body, what was going on with it, or how to fix it. Without Zoloft keeping a lid on my emotions they were like a geyser spewing everywhere. I'd gone from a high-ish dose 150mg/daily to 0mg with no new tools, resources, or professional support. Please don't go off medication without supervision, loads of tools and resources, and really liking and believing in your reason for going off.

I had wave after wave of panic attacks that evening and for about three months. With each one I thought, "This will be the one that kills me. God, I hope Sully and the dogs know how much I love them!" My heart goes out to everyone who has had, or currently has them. They fucking suck and can made me feel powerless, broken, and like something was very wrong with me.

My background alarm had been set off by a perfect storm of events and I didn't know how to help myself. There were many days after my dark night that I didn't want to wake up. Not because I wanted to die, but because I knew what the day was probably going to feel like. I had to cancel work appointments because I just couldn't force myself to do it. Each morning my wife came up with to-do lists so I wouldn't lay in bed all day, be anxious about anxiety, and ruminate. In order to keep moving forward, Dory's phrase from *Finding Nemo*, was on repeat in my mind, "Just keep swimming, just keep swimming." It helped a lot, thanks little fishy.

Taking a shower, brushing my teeth, and running a comb through my hair were like trying to climb Mt. Everest in flip-flops. A "good" day was determined by if I felt "up to" putting earrings on. I'd ask myself, "Is it an earring day Jenn?" Some were and some weren't. I felt so fucking broken and worried that I may not be able to work anymore. I felt like a shell of a human and was in a constant state of alarm.

I believe my high-ish dose of Zoloft, as well as alcohol and processed sugar, were keeping a lid on unprocessed trauma stored in my body. And the combo of not being on it, and what-ever was jarred loose in my alarm system the night I smoked pot, allowed the trauma, emotions, and feelings to flood my ill-equipped system.

I saw my therapist a lot. Twice a week for a month, slowly moving to once or twice a month. During this crazy ass dumpster fire of a season, I found life coaching, somatic practices, and learned a lot about how we store trauma in our bodies. I'm grateful for this priceless information because they're helping me heal what I can and can't remember from my childhood, instead of just putting band-aids on the symptoms.

I reached out to friends and was honest about what I was going through. It felt good to be real with them and allow myself to receive their support, which isn't easy for me.

A couple years after this happened and I was feeling more stable with my new-found tools and support. I felt a nudge to lower my dose of Zoloft a smidge because I felt blocked emotionally. I felt like a statue which isn't how I want to live. I've worked hard, especially since 2018, to learn how to support and show up for myself, which means tending to my body's alarm and not trying to think my way out of its messages and warnings. I felt like I was in a good place and was open to processing more of life's ups and downs and whatever else my soul and spirit felt it was time to address.

I made an appointment with my doctor, who happened not to be the same one who had me go off Zoloft, and we had a long discussion about what I was wanting to do and why. I'm so grateful for all her support–thanks Dr. Debra Boyce, you're a great physician! I only went down 25mg, because I believe in kitten steps with all things. I noticed a few more "feelings" and was totally ok with that because I'd loaded my toolbox with all the things I've included in this book. I only suggest things I practice and find helpful.

About a year later, I talked to my doctor again because I was ready to kitten-step down another 25mg. We lowered it again, and I'm going to hang out here for the foreseeable future. I'm not trying to go off it. I'm listening to, and acting on, what feels good for me.

This journey has been a wild one! It was my dark night of the soul and I've come out the other side with more tools, smarts, and evidence that we can't exclude the body when we're taking care of our mental health. They're inextricable and we can't think our way out of a feeling problem.

CHAPTER 9

Our Brains Have Alarm Systems

I read an email from marketing "shenious," Hillary Weiss, that stopped me in my tracks. She attended a business-y event, and someone asked her the following question that stopped her in her tracks. So much track stopping.

The question was: What is it you don't want us to see?

To quote my people in North Dakota, "Uff da!" That gets me right between the eyes and right in the gut. And cue my deer-in-the-headlight look.

I don't want you to see/know that sometimes my internal alarm goes off when Sully has a couple cocktails. I don't want you to know that I'm 48 years old and have a few inner children. Yep, we have more than one, who get "alarmed" by these old and deep childhood wounds of growing up in an alcoholic home.

I like the term *alarmed* because I think it accurately describes a coping mechanism that serves us in childhood but can be maladaptive in adulthood. My reactions have caused arguments between us and we've both created emotional armor over the years. This is an onion with lots of layers and I'm tending to them. Slowly, gently, and compassionately.

My alarm looks and feels like:

- A heightened sense of alertness to anything that seems off.
- I literally don't feel like I'm 48 years old. I feel like I'm 16 years old and wondering what condition my dad is going to be in.

- My breathing is shallower.
- I'm hypersensitive to her words and actions, trying to detect anything that might seem "dangerous" to my nervous system. These are very old feelings because I've never been in danger with my wife.
- I've picked fights to "prove myself right" when there really wasn't anything to be upset about.
- My shoulders raise without realizing it until it's happened.
- I catch my fingers and butt muscles tensing.

I want to be a cool wife who's easy breezy about all the things. But sometimes I'm not. That wound has been there, and I've been working on it since *long* before I met my wife. It has nothing to do with her, per se, it's me. I've also created a multi-layered shame sandwich for not "fixing" this yet, which has only made it more difficult to release, let go of, and heal.

The more awareness and compassion I give to my alarm/inner kids, the more they feel like they can chill, and don't have to rush up to protect me. Awareness and compassion are beautiful salves to our souls, and they're unsung "heroes." They're underutilized tools because they seem passive and not forceful enough to get the job done. Screw that.

I'm entering a new phase of being/healing. I can feel it in my bones. The more I tend to my body when its alarm is going off, and soothe it without shame, the closer I get to healing that alarmed/anxious part, and it can stand down because it feels safer. The more I work with my body's sensations to release the old stuck trauma energy/alarm/anxiety, the more present I can be as the 48-year-old that I am.

The more I let go of shaming and judging myself for being exactly where I am, the closer I get to healing that wounded part of me. Shaming and judging haven't helped, and boy howdy did

I try. Impatience hasn't helped. Denying how I'm feeling hasn't helped. They've only kept me stuck, treading in muddy water with all sorts of things just waiting to bite my toes.

The more I acknowledge and talk about the alarm that goes into protective mode, and practice listening to her instead of beating her down, the more healing takes place. We all have alarms. It's a part of humaning. The alarm in me honors the alarm in you.

How do you know when you're in alarm? Answering this will require curiosity, and hindsight in the beginning. Curiosity, because it's really easy to shame and judge ourselves, but those old hats will only keep you where you're at the moment. And hindsight, because in the beginning we don't realize what we're doing, and we need to take a peek backwards to evaluate.

Please put on your scientist or detective "hat." We're going to look at the facts, not the stew of emotions you may have been swimming in. This is where we get to practice decreasing our levels of shame and judgment. It's really easy to go down a spiral of shame about all the "bad, awful, terrible, embarrassing, or cringe-worthy" things we've done when we're alarmed. You've done that enough, Sunshine, we aren't going to do that now.

Is there an old behavior, response, pattern, or habit that isn't serving you? Name it. Be as honest with yourself as you can about it. We can't change what we don't acknowledge. We need to shine a light of compassion on it. These all start sometime in childhood as coping mechanisms. They can serve us when we're little, but don't when we're adults:

- You might react without any conscious awareness of what you're doing.
- Have another glass of wine or grab some chocolate to try to soothe yourself.

- Your reaction might be "bigger" than what's warranted for that situation. I do this when my younger parts feel shushed.
- Get passive/aggressive when you wanted to say something but felt like you couldn't.
- You might not feel like "yourself." That's a sign that I'm acting from a younger part of me that's trying to be protective.
- You want to shut down or shut the situation down.

Being on high alert 24/7 served me as a kid in a home with lots of drinking. It kept me on my toes, gave me a false sense of control, and helped me feel like I was a step ahead of the chaos. Today, I can see the wisdom and brilliance of what my kiddo alarm was doing. I can send love and compassion to my alarm/younger self. She was a fucking rock star. She was trying to protect me and keep me safe. And it worked. I'm a relatively well-adjusted 48-year-old adult. Thank you, little Jenny.

Being in a constant state of alarm doesn't serve me as an adult. I'm working on becoming aware of it when it goes off, dropping down into my body, doing one of the somatic practices discussed in this book. The volume of my alarm *is* going down. My inner kiddo *is* feeling safer in her body.

The primitive part of our brains doesn't know the difference between past, present, and future. When we're remembering something or thinking about the future, your brain thinks you're experiencing the thing right now. That's why you can logically know that you're safe now, but it doesn't register in your body and brain. They're reacting as if you're experiencing the memory, or future thing, now.

I will continue to show up for my alarm/little Jenny and help my brain to continue to rewire itself. That's what I'm doing by breaking the cycle of constant alarm. I'm not broken or damaged — and neither are you. The pathways in my brain became wired to react a certain way when I experienced the stuff I did in childhood. And now I know it's my responsibility to see what isn't working and make changes. It's not my fault, and it is my responsibility to change it if I want things to be different.

That's the reality.

I can piss and moan, place blame, or throw people under the bus, but at the end of the day, it's my life and my responsibility to change it. No one's gonna save me, fix it, or make the necessary changes. Those have to come from me. It isn't anyone else's job or responsibility. So, I'm asking for support, getting coaching and therapy, and practicing giving myself truckloads of awareness and compassion as I sometimes faceplant and skin my knees along the way.

When I first posted this on social media, I was amazed at how much lighter I felt. Not that we need to put all the things on our chosen platforms. That's what I felt called to do. Once it was out there, I felt so much less shame and judgment. My load was lighter because I wasn't carrying around a secret.

That secret and its shame and judgment kept me in a self-induced cage, and I could feel it in my bones that it was time to bust out. If I didn't break out of the cage, I ran the risk of staying there for the rest of my life and I was tired of playing it safe and small. Being able to get to the next level in my life was only going to happen if I set myself free.

Having an alarm or other unhelpful response comes with being a human. It's ok. We can tend to them and quiet their volume.

CHAPTER 10

Anxiety is Normal

When I was in the process of putting this book together, I had written a fair amount about anxiety. It was sprinkled in many of the chapters. Like most of my coaching clients, I experienced a lot of anxiety: think low-grade hypervigilance 24/7. It felt like the worst constant companion you could imagine. I *hated* it in every way possible. I saw it as a flaw and my nemesis. I hated my brain for having this problem and said more than once to my coaches and therapists, "Can I *please* just have a lobotomy and get a new brain?!"

I thought my life would be so much better if I could just *figure this anxiety thing out*. And I tried. Boy oh boy did I try. I tried:

- Positive affirmations
- Ignoring it
- Stuffing it down with food
- Washing it down with wine
- Reading every book I could get my hands on that looked promising
- Listening to podcasts
- Working out
- Lots of talk therapy
- Ignoring it (did I already say that?)
- Coaching
- Journaling
- Trying to out-think my thoughts
- Praying to all the things for help and guidance

- White knuckling it
- Somatic practices (connecting to your body to ground and center yourself)
- And loads more trying to think my way out of the hell I was in

Pieces and parts of the above list helped me, no doubt about it! A handful of them are still in my self-care bucket today! Namely: books, podcasts, working out, coaching, therapy, and somatic practices.

If I had a dollar for every time I said or wrote that anxiety is a normal human emotion, my family could afford homes on both coasts of the United States and at least one in Europe. And a private jet to get us there.

Then I read Dr. Russell Kennedy's book, *Anxiety Rx: A New Prescription for Anxiety Relief from the Doctor Who Created It.* I love the way Dr. Kennedy easily describes anxiety and has simple body and brain-based solutions. His book is a must-read. He was the first person to liken what most of us call anxiety to an alarm that's going off in our bodies. It was a "holy shit that's me!" moment. That feeling of alarm has been my experience my entire life. That's what I've called anxiety.

Dr. Kennedy says, "Think of a headache right now. Does that thought hurt? Anxious thoughts are the same: the thought itself doesn't hurt. The pain you're feeling is a sense of alarm in your body, and that *is* painful... I am defining anxiety and breaking it down into its component parts- anxious thoughts in the mind and (an) alarmed feeling in the body."

When I heard that I was floored. It was like someone actually described it exactly how I've experienced it my entire life. I'd never felt so seen or heard.

The other key component in Dr. Kennedy's book is how he

says, "You can't think your way out of a feeling problem." For the love of all things good and holy; that's 99.9% of the things I've tried. I believed, hoped, prayed that I could *think* or outsmart my way out of anxiety, but it doesn't work that way. If it did, no one would experience anxiety because most of us are constantly thinking and living in our heads.

We're in our heads so much because at some point in our lives, consciously or unconsciously, we learned we weren't safe in our bodies, so we retreated to "safer" territory: our minds.

While in our bodies some of us experienced:

- Physical abuse
- Parents who drank too much, took drugs, were workaholics, or traveled constantly
- Being yelled at by their parents or their parents fighting with each other
- Sexual abuse
- Emotional, physical, or spiritual neglect
- A sibling or parent was sick
- A general sense of not being safe in your home
- Another sibling was clearly favored

Dr. Kennedy goes on to explain, "Anxiety is an early warning system that is trying to help you survive but goes rogue. It's not there to harm you, but in its constant warnings, it makes you feel unsafe. Chronic worry is a maladaptive coping strategy, not a disease." You are not broken, and you are not alone. While very painful, it all makes perfect sense that you're "anxious" or a worrier. You are very normal and in very good and abundant company!

The best news is that no matter what your past looked like, your present and future can look very different. No more trying to think your way out of anxiety because it doesn't work.

We can't keep trying to think our way out of a feeling problem and expect to get any traction. What does work is tending to, loving on, and showing up for your inner alarm that are actually younger versions of you that didn't get what they needed. But I'm going to teach you how to show up for them like a boss, in a gentle and compassionate way, of course.

If you grew up with one or more of the above bullet-pointed experiences, I bet your nervous system/alarm is easily activated, and/or is on 24/7 like mine was.

The thing about retreating to our minds for "safety'" is that it usually isn't safer up there. It's usually scarier because of our anxious thoughts. It's imperative that we slowly and gently reconnect with our bodies because that's where the alarm lives and that's where it can be tended to. We can't live from the neck up anymore if we want to heal our anxiety.

I've made a lot of headway in healing my alarm/anxiety. I'm nowhere near the places I've been in the past which included panic attacks, not having difficult conversations, not speaking up for myself, and staying small in countless ways. Now I'm more comfortable in social situations, I started a podcast in 2021, now I feel more comfortable in my skin than I ever have, and there have been some nice long breaks where I don't feel the alarm at all.

A part of me has always known that I was going to have to make friends with my body again if I wanted to live a full life. Making friends as an adult can be awkward no matter who it is. I was going to have to go to the places that scared me instead of ignoring them for the rest of my life. For me it started with deciding to stop drinking alcohol, then I knew it was time to cut way back on processed sugar because both were my coping mechanisms and keeping me from the work I knew I needed to do.

I feel so much freer, lighter, and expansive with my updated perspective on anxiety/alarm. It feels true in my bones, and I feel capable of helping heal the younger parts of me who have only been trying to protect me this whole time. They can take a break from their 24/7 watchdog duties and go play kickball, color, roller skate, or go to the park with friends.

CHAPTER 11

Ditch Labels

I find most labels unhelpful. Like the ones on pints of ice cream or bags of chips. Give me a URL to look it up if I want, but don't put the calorie count in an extra big font where I can see it plain as day. That's just unnecessary and rude. Mind 'ya business and let me eat in peace thankyouverymuch.

Other labels are just as unhelpful. Depressed, anxious, angry, and selfish to name a few. They put a negative blanket over the whole person. They personify our experiences. They oversimplify the complexity of who we are.

We are not our emotions or feelings. They are 90 second experiences of energy passing *through* us. Not who we *are*.

The distinction is imperative; I really want you to see it, and let it sink in.

You, the awesome person reading or listening to this book, are not depression, the number on a scale, anxiety, anger, or grief. You experience them, but they are not you. You are the amazing essence left after you strip away your heavy labels, shitty beliefs, and fucked up expectations that we all carry around every day.

We slap labels on ourselves left and right without thinking about the bigger picture and all the things that could be contributing to a normal response to a hard situation. We want to quickly name the problem so we can try to get to a fast and easy solution. The primitive human brain likes the efficiency of labels. It can put a label on it and then work to find the answer. It wants to keep everything neat and tidy, so you have energy to fight off tigers and bears.

Except there aren't always quick and easy solutions to our emotions...and that's ok. It's going to take a hot minute to get curious and unpack what's going on, and then take some kitten steps to support yourself. It's more than possible and it won't take long. Per usual, Sunshine, I got you!

All of our feelings and emotions are normal responses to perceived potential danger. Our primitive brains are doing exactly what they have evolved to do over the 650 million years that our species has been on the planet.

We don't go around saying, "I'm a joyful person or I'm a grieving person," but we also have those feelings as humans. We do it with the ones that are deemed negative. Labeling myself or someone else with a fleeting emotion doesn't serve us, and neither does knowing how many calories are in the pint of ice cream or bag of chips I'm going to eat.

Thanks to actor Kristen Bell and some wisdom she shared on a podcast, I changed the *story* I tell myself and others, and *how* I talk about my feelings. She said about herself, "I'm a person who sometimes feels anxiety," instead of labeling herself as anxious. Mic drop!

We are supposed to have a wide range of emotions because we have a wide range of thoughts. That's ok and as it should be. But we pathologize and resist our feelings, which allows them to perpetuate instead of us getting curious about them, feeling them, and letting them move through you. We make it a bad thing to feel anxiety, depressed, grief, or heavier than you'd like to be. We think the negative label will help us change. It never does though. It only adds shame and keeps us stuck.

Kristen's brilliant distinction helped me see that *I* am not what I'm *feeling*, and that nothing was wrong with me when I was feeling anxiety as a kid. I wasn't broken, defective, or flawed because of my emotions. I was a healthy human experiencing normal responses to jacked up circumstances. The labels added so much unnecessary shame and suffering to my life.

Labels hold us back from what we want out of our beautiful and precious lives, because of what we think that label means about us. Pick one of your labels and say it to yourself now. How does your body feel, and what does it do? Does it shrink or recoil, do you feel shame?

If so, it's time to put on your compassionate glasses and have a looksie at what's up. It's time to have a 30,000-feet view and start ditching the labels. They were never the truth, and it's time to dissolve them because they're constricting your awesomeness and shine!

When you get curious about your labels and cut back on using them, you'll:

- See your response is normal for your experiences, not your totality as a person.
- Ditch your old, stinky, and moldy story about yourself.
- Suddenly want to go to an arcade or pick up an old interest that used to make you smile.
- Feel lighter, freer, more expansive, hopeful, powerful, energetic, and optimistic.
- Feel a connection to your authentic self, inner essence, spark, and effervescence.
- Want to connect or reconnect with your favorite peeps.
- Want to have more fun and be playful.

What amazing things could happen if you ripped off your labels and burned them?!

What would you say, do, think, try, without the labels?!

What kind of spaciousness would it create inside you?!

What would you let go of?!

Ditch the labels, Sunshine, they're dulling your sparkle!

CHAPTER 12

Calm Social Anxiety

Social anxiety?

I hear 'ya. I feel 'ya. I know 'ya. I see 'ya.

Groups of people, and anticipating being around groups of people, used to be more than enough to activate the alarm in my nervous system. I'd have all sorts of worries going through my melon. "Who's going to be there, how's it going to go, will I run out of things to talk about, will I be interesting, how will I handle awkward silences?" Ahhhhh! This is when I used to head for the booze or desserts, LOL!

So much worry before and during get togethers. So many feelings of discomfort. So many memories of middle and high school, and all the while my primitive brain was telling me I would die from all the feelings. Contrary to my previous beliefs, booze, and desserts did not make things easier. They just made me feel terrible after.

So, what's a human to do when they find themselves in these situations, with these feelings?

Get curious.

Ask your brain and body what's going on? What are they thinking? Where is your body feeling the alarm? And what would help them feel safer aside from running away? Although sometimes that is the best thing, but not usually.

- Check in with a safe person or hangout with a friendly pet for a few moments. Physical contact will co-regulate and calm your nervous system.

- Go to the bathroom and do three physiological sighs (described in chapter 65) or any of the somatic practices in this book.
- Practice being with the discomfort for 10 seconds before taking another trip to the desserts.
- Feel your feet on the floor and remind your sweet brain of the thousands of similar situations you've lived through.
- Ask yourself if you are safe in this moment or in the next five seconds? And then keep asking and affirming that you are.

I still get a little "alarmy" in social situations, but I've really been able to show up for myself more and turn down the volume of the anxiety. I don't have to do anything perfectly, nor do I need to try to "get rid" of the anxiety. It can come along for the ride, and I don't need to make it a problem.

CHAPTER 13

Am I Safe in This Moment?

A few years ago, I had a string of panic attacks, and it was suggested that I repeat the phrase, "I am safe, I am safe, I am safe…"

There was only one *huge* problem with that. My brain and body felt anything but safe and I didn't believe a damn word I was saying.

So repeating that phrase over and over was not only not helping, it was keeping me on high alert, because every time I'd say it, my brain and body would reply with, "The hell you are, so we're gonna keep our eyes peeled!"

I've learned a tweaked version of that phrase that actually helps soothe my nervous system and quiets my alarm when it goes off.

In Dr. Russell Kennedy's book, *Anxiety Rx,* he suggests asking ourselves, "Am I safe in this moment? Am I safe in the next five seconds?" Those questions help ground and calm us in our bodies in the present moment, instead of us spinning out in past regret or future worry. They also help us use our brains for us instead of against us. They pull us out of our alarm and primitive brain, and into our rational prefrontal cortex.

Answer those questions to yourself or out loud as many times as you'd like to reinforce your safety in the present moment. This continues to show your precious brain and body that you are actually safe.

It's also a great idea to do this throughout your day to build a stronger general feeling of safety in your body which is so important for those of us who haven't felt safe or comfortable in our bodies for a variety of reasons.

You totally got this, Sunshine *and* you, are, safe! <3

CHAPTER 14

Counter Spin

When my internal alarm goes off, my brain starts to spin and spiral. It's like being on a merry-go-round that's going too fast to safely jump off without face planting and skinning my knees and palms. It sucks because I feel helpless to get out of it, and as stuck as a fly on a sticky strip in the summer by a trash can.

But I have another tool for you that I use regularly when I notice I'm slipping, or have slipped, into a "spin cycle." I learned it from Melissa Tiers. She calls it the counter spin.

- Close your eyes and for just a moment, tap into the spinning energy, and notice the direction it's spinning. You may notice your body naturally follows the spin.
- Open your eyes and take your pointer finger from one hand and mimic the spin just in front of you, close to your body. Do that for a few seconds.
- Then take your finger that's mimicking the spin and while keeping it spinning, extend your hand to arm's length in front of you. Do that for a few seconds.
- Next, reverse the spin to the opposite direction while your hand is extended. Do that for a few seconds.
- Then while spinning in the opposite direction, bring your finger back close to your body and then laugh. Yes, you read that right. Laugh like you just read the funniest meme ever.

The counter spin disrupts the neurons that have fired together in our brain that are causing the spin, often for decades, and allows our nervous system the chance to calm down. It disrupts the "anxiety spin" so you can decide what to do next from your prefrontal cortex, that creative and executive functioning part of our brain, instead of our fight-flight-freeze area. The counter spin interrupts the well-worn path that our patterns of alarm and anxious thoughts have created in our brains and allows different neurons to fire together and then wire together, to create a new default non-spinny pattern. The laugh at the end reinforces to your brain that you're safe, which "seals in" the positive rewiring.

Practice, practice, practice. Start with something small, not necessarily your biggest stressor, and just keep practicing. The more we practice these tools the better we are truly, honestly, and genuinely taking care of ourselves, and creating lasting positive change for ourselves and everyone around us. You are rewiring your brain each time you practice!

CHAPTER 15

My Gray Area Drinking

I didn't have my first drop of alcohol until I was 20. It was a Zima with a lime, hello 1994.

Because a lot of people in my family of origin and extended family were heavy drinkers, I didn't want to touch the stuff. I told myself, "instant alcoholic, just add alcohol." That wasn't exactly the case for me. I drank occasionally when I was 20 and went to the bars with friends when I turned 21, but didn't drink much.

I never got a DUI although I did drive after I'd been drinking which I completely regret. Goes to show our judgment is impaired after a few beverages even though we think it isn't.

I was never injured because I'd been drinking. I never fell, cut myself, or fell out of bed, etc.

No one ever sat me down and had a conversation with me about my drinking.

I never missed work because I was hungover.

If you asked anyone close to me, they'd say I was a "normal" drinker.

But I didn't like *why* I drank, how my mood quickly changed, and especially how I felt physically and mentally the next day after having two glasses of wine.

I drank because that's what most adults do. It's "normal" to drink alcohol. It's the only substance that you're questioned about if you *don't* do it. "Are you pregnant, taking medication, what's wrong?" I drank because I wanted to be part of the "fun" and didn't want to feel left out. We're pack animals and we want to do what our pack is doing. That's a 650-million-year-old pattern that takes a hot minute to rewire.

I drank because it relaxed me. For a few minutes. Most people know alcohol is a depressant, but it has a flip side that most people aren't aware of. Shortly after our first sips, our bodies notice something's off, we're out of balance, and our bodies don't like that. We're depressed from the depressant, so our brilliant bodies send adrenaline and cortisol into our systems, two stress hormones. Because we have a jolt of stress hormones, our bodies feel a little more anxious so we have another drink to calm down. Most of us are unaware of this vicious cycle.

I drank because I had a hard day and it was a reward. An adult version of getting a sticker, or cake pop. I drank because I "earned" it. Adulting is hard, and we're trained by advertisers that you "deserve a break," and drinking is just the thing that'll make everything better, easier, and less difficult to deal with. Or so they said.

I drank because it helped me not feel my internal alarm, think anxious thoughts, or feel my feelings for a little while. My brain would quiet down its chatter and incessant yammering. Alcohol impedes cognitive function so, sure it did quiet my brain chatter, but it didn't make my problems go away or any easier to deal with the next day. Wine and Costco margaritas just made me feel foggy and beat myself up for numbing myself instead of finding a legit solution or sitting with my feelings for 90 seconds until they moved through.

I drank because it was a habit. It's what I did when I came home. I'd say hey to my wife and dogs, hang up my keys, put on my comfy clothes, and pour a glass of cold Chardonnay. I had created the pattern in my brain. It was almost unconscious.

But I didn't like how I felt after a few sips. The first sip of a cold, buttery Chardonnay, or a well-made margarita with a squeeze of lime, was divine. I would feel a warm wash of relaxation come over me. "There you are, that's better…"

Pretty soon I'd notice a little irritability, sassiness, a disregard for better choices, "sure I'll have another glass" or, "yes, a big sugary dessert sounds great!"

I didn't feel like *me*. I felt like a duller, snippy, sometimes loud and emotionally immature version of myself. I didn't like not remembering every moment of the evening, or wondering if I said something I normally wouldn't.

I didn't like that version of myself. It was a half-assed version. My shine was half of what it usually is and I carried around a low-grade yuck of feeling like crap about myself. It was like wearing a weighted blanket all the time and wondering why I felt so blah and heavy.

I didn't like how I felt after I drank. I wouldn't feel rested because it completely screws with our sleep cycles and doesn't allow us to get deep or restorative sleep. I'd wake up a few times, struggle to get back to sleep, curse my alarm when it went off, and drag my ass all day.

My brain would be in a fog, not at all clear and ready to meet the day with a spring in my step. If I worked out the next morning it was a slog. My legs would feel heavy, like I was trying to move in freshly poured cement. It was hard to take good deep breaths. It just sucked all around and made me dislike working out which I actually love doing.

Because I had this low-grade self-hate and fog/slog going on, I didn't make food choices that fueled me. I'd go for the hard salami and sharp cheddar cheese sandwich on white bread with butter and a side of Cheetos instead of the salad I freaking love.

The thought, "I did this to myself *again*," and the self-loathing that accompanied, didn't make me the best person to be around. I don't know that it was noticeable to anyone other than Sully occasionally, but I wasn't the person I wanted to be, and am now.

In May of 2018, the morning after a friend's annual party, I was in the bathroom getting sick after drinking too much. With my head over the toilet I asked myself out loud if this was how I wanted to live my life. The answer was a hard hell no! I was wasting my precious life's energy, time, and feeling like crap emotionally and physically.

Five months later, in October of 2018, I decided to take a break from alcohol and just see what happend. Because there *had* to be a better way to live. A life lived at full volume instead of half or two-thirds.

I was nervous to tell Sully about my decision because we drank together, it was a shared activity, and I was nervous about her reaction. She was totally supportive when I told her. I know not everyone gets that reaction and I'm very grateful to her.

I had a lot of mind drama. And questions:

- Could I go more than a few nights without wine? Even thinking about going one night made me nervous. Turns out I can go a lotta nights without it.
- What the hell would that be like? Uncomfortable at first, very enjoyable after that.
- What will I drink when we go out? Club soda with a lime please.
- What will other people think? Ninety-nine percent of people in my life didn't say one word because I'm not surrounded by assholes, and because usually the only people concerned with someone not drinking, is someone concerned about their own drinking.
- Will I still have fun? OMG yes, and more actually! And I feel good the next day, not like roadkill, and I remember everything I said and did.

- Will other people annoy me when they drink? Sometimes, because drunk people can be annoying. I know I was.

I had to practice sitting with the discomfort and feelings I'd pushed down because they were surfacing. That happens when you take away the thing you're using to hold stuff down. I expected that, and tried to be open to it. I was done running. I had to practice showing up for myself and addressing what my body, mind, and spirit were really looking for instead of what I thought was at the bottom of a glass of wine.

Sometimes that looked like placing one hand on my heart and the other on my belly to soothe my body's alarm. I didn't die. Not once. Even though my primitive brain kept telling me I might. I kept talking sweetly back to it, thanking it for its warning and moving in the direction I wanted to go. Which was to not feel like alcohol had power over me and that life would suck without it.

I did it slowly and intentionally for three years.

I never worried about the word or label of alcoholic because I don't think it's helpful or serves me. I did spend time Googling, "what's an alcoholic?" We can do ourselves a huge disservice by trying to figure out if we are, or not, instead of just asking ourselves if it's worth it to keep alcohol in our lives. Is it "taking" more than it's "giving." Answer that question and move on.

At the end of the day alcohol wasn't serving me, or adding anything positive to my life. It was really taking away from my life, and I wasn't ok with that anymore.

Then after a little over three years of not drinking, and a lot of thought, I made the conscious decision to have a glass of wine. I guess I wanted to see if all the above was still true. I drank for about one-and-a-half years with the same results.

Turns out, I was right the first time. By drinking alcohol, I was dimming my light. I was cutting myself off at the knees. I was keeping myself small and living at half volume. And that's not what I came here to do.

On January 20, 2022, I told Sully I was done for good. That I was right the first time.

Life is messy. It's not black and white or linear, although our brains would love that so much because they equate those things with safety.

I've heard similar drinking experiences called "gray area drinking," because it doesn't have huge consequences and treatment isn't involved. I didn't hit a messy or awful "bottom." It was a self-imposed bottom, a line I drew in the sand.

It's the gray area. Like when you have blood work and the results come back in the "normal range" but they're too low or high for your specific chemistry.

I'm grateful my story didn't have a tragic twist or ending. I'm grateful I listened to the voice in my heart/gut that kept telling me that there's a better way to live, and it's 100% within my reach if I do the work.

"Cheers," with a club soda and lime!

CHAPTER 16

The "Why" of Addiction

Over the years my thoughts and beliefs change as I learn and experience new things. I don't ever want to dig in my heels and not be open to new ideas. This has definitely been the case with the subject of addiction. The word itself can evoke so many strong thoughts and feelings. We all have unique experiences that determine our viewpoints and I wanted to share mine with you as I see it today.

Some people see addiction/dependence/overuse as a flaw in their character. A weakness, a damaged chromosome in their DNA, or that they somehow drew the short straw. Others see it as a disease. And the newest perspective I've come across is that there's a deep wisdom and intelligence to our addictive behaviors.

In this chapter I'm going to talk about my experiences growing up in a home with two heavy drinkers and how I used food, and later alcohol, to try to soothe myself. I'm going to explain some science-y stuff that happens in human brains when we partake in these behaviors and show you that we're wired to do these things. We aren't broken; this is our wiring, and there are solutions. Here we go.

Our spidey senses are on point even as kids. We may not have the words to describe a situation or our feelings about it, but we are very aware that something is off.

As a kid, I didn't know the words addiction or alcoholic. I only knew my parents drank "too much," loud and scary things happened when they did, and this didn't happen in my friends' homes. They were lucky.

I used birthday wishes and "lucky" pennies to try to get my parents to stop drinking. I prayed, tried to be perfect every way I could think of, and felt like I should be able to *do something* to get them to quit. It never occurred to me that it was out of my control. I thought there *had* to be something I could do, so I'll just keep trying harder. My little kid brain did not and could not accept the realities that I couldn't and that it wasn't my job or responsibility. I couldn't accept "defeat."

I didn't know until recently that it's too much for our young and fragile attachments to our caregivers to let go of trying to fix them. The "dance" and "addiction" relationship I had with my parents was a tether that kept us connected. It would've crushed me to see that the responsibility and ball was in their court. I already felt alone and like I was raising myself. I needed that tether even if it was an illusion.

I was very ashamed of their drinking and behavior and *hated* that there wasn't a damn thing I could do about it. I also felt dirty and weighed down by this family secret. It was like carrying around a weighted blanket all the time. It never occurred to me that the blanket wasn't mine to carry, worry about, or try to fix. I took it on because if it's my responsibility to fix, then there's something I can do about it. I'm in control. This is a newer realization for me and has shown up in other areas of my life like my health. If I'm responsible, I'm in control.

I had my own issues and challenges with food and sugar starting in fourth grade. I broke my right leg jumping off my school's stage and had a cast on from my foot to my crotch for four weeks. I was a really active kid, riding my bike and playing with my friends in the neighborhood, and the cast put the kibosh on that. I snacked on Cheetos, Oreos, Mountain Dew, and candy to fill the loneliness.

In no time, those foods became my "quick fixes" when I

wanted/needed something to make me feel better when my parents would fight, or I'd notice my mom's Huntington's Disease symptoms getting stronger or more noticeable, felt left out of something at school, or basically to avoid any thoughts and feelings I didn't want to experience. Period.

I would sneak food so no one in my family would notice. Like rearrange the Oreos in the container my mom put them in, "fluff up" the chip bags so they looked fuller, hide and eat canned cake frosting in our basement, go through DQ's drive through in another area of town and eat a large blizzard as I drove around, eat slices of white bread until my stomach was so full and I'd basically drop the slice on the floor that I couldn't finish, and pass out. It was a really painful period in my life.

I often thought about trying to make myself throw up after a binge but didn't, so all that extra food showed up on my body. I was overweight, plain and simple. My life and brain felt like they were totally out of control.

One night when I was about 14 or 15, I had some kind of stomach bug and needed to get to the bathroom. I was feeling pretty weak so my dad helped me to the bathroom. The next morning when I came out of my room, my dad was waiting for me and I saw the bathroom scale in the middle of the living room. He told me to get on it. Through tears I begged him to not make me do it but it didn't work. He got on the scale first because he wanted to compare our weights. Then I got on. I don't remember the numbers but our weights were close, and I remember thinking and saying to myself that I'm never going to let that happen again or feel that crushing humiliation again.

The next morning I began severely restricting what I ate, and exercising constantly. It was a big, "Fuck you!" to my dad. I barely ate more than 500 calories a day and would ride my bike to and from the gym to workout. A few times in the summer heat I remember thinking I hope I don't pass out and crash my bike. The anger I felt towards my dad fueled my actions for about a year. I took up running, which is totally not me, but I loved the runner's high and how many calories I could burn when I ran in the heat. What was under the anger was a huge well of hurt that I wasn't willing or able to process.

I remember going back to school my junior year and some of the popular girls started talking to me. I was like, "Oh wow, they want to talk to me now that I've lost 50 pounds, yay me, bonus!"

I could only keep up the food restricting and over exercising for about a year. I started eating all the things again. I felt so messed up in the head and out of control again that I joined O.A., Overeaters Anonymous, when I was 16. I met my best friend there and that's the best thing that came out of it for me. Many of the meetings felt like we were treading water in the problem, stuck in the muck, and I didn't like that. It felt gross and like I was walking around with this life sentence of food/sugar addict. I kept asking myself and my BFF, "Ok so what do we do about it, where are the solutions because I'm well aware of the problem?" I attended meetings for about three years but quit going because I felt worse after going, not better. I realize that some folks love 12-Step meetings, you do you boo, they just weren't my cup of tea.

Fast forward through my 20s and 30s and I'm not even sure how it happened, but I just wasn't binging like I used to. Maybe it was starting to sink in that that path was going to lead to more pain than sitting with the yucky thoughts and feelings. I still felt like crap but I wasn't treating my body like a garbage disposal and dealing with as many extra layers of shame and judgment.

In my early 40s I was beginning to think I didn't have a good relationship with alcohol. A few times I'd Google something like, "How do I know if I'm an alcoholic? Or What is addictive behavior?" All those questions got me was spinning in circles asking questions that really didn't matter at the end of the day. The best questions I've ever heard about any behavior that you're wondering about are, is it worth it to keep this in my life? And what is it costing me to keep it in my life? Those questions made things very clear for me and kept me from going down time and energy wasting rabbit holes.

In 2022 I took a class on Shame with Simone Seol and David Bedrick that really changed how I look at addiction. In the past I saw addiction as a flaw, thanks in part to what was drilled in my brain while I was in a 12-step program, "It's a character defect." So I believed that about myself and others. There's just this part that's broken and different from those who don't have an addiction. Blech, that's such a grossly oversimplified, black and white, shitty myopic way to look at something that's complex and layered. It didn't feel right to believe that about myself and others but when you're told that over and over and over, it sticks.

David introduced me to the idea that there's an intelligence to addictions. Remember that our primitive brains always want to protect us from pain, physical and emotional. They also want to increase our pleasure and do everything as efficiently as possible. And what's a more efficient way to do that than anything that falls into the broad definition of an addiction?

- Rough day at the office? Go home and have some wine.
- Kids drove you bonkers at bedtime? Have a sleeve of Oreos.
- MIL said the thing about your parenting style? Buy everything in your Amazon cart.
- Had a fight with your spouse? Speed scroll on all the socials.

Nothing is wrong with any of those "solutions" unless they're your go-to when any shit hits any fan. And even then, they are giving you a message that something's off and needs to be tended to. They're like warning flares, waving flags, the check engine lights in your car. They're your cues that your nervous system/alarm needs and wants to be taken care of. But it's just a habit to reach for the quick and easy thing because it "relieves" the pain and increases your pleasure really fast.

See the intelligence? You feel like crap and the wine, sugar, Amazon, and your phone are quick and easy fixes that your brain has learned over the years. It's freaking genius if we look at it from a 30,000-foot view and take the emotion away! I started by talking to my cravings for sugar. Asking them what was going on for them. What did they need and want? And I got answers. I just needed to be willing to listen and listen to them from a place of curiosity instead of trying to destroy and get rid of them.

Our primitive brains are wired for our survival, not our happiness. They've learned that reaching for one of those "solutions" will keep you alive. They don't care that they also make you miserable from the hangover, stuffed stomach, high credit card balance, or wasted time staring at our screens. You made yourself "feel better" and are alive, so your primitive brain sees that as a win for you. It doesn't care that you're now beating yourself up and feeling like shit.

This is where it's important to start to see the intelligence. At this point in my life, and only with lots of practice, I can look at my parents' drinking and see that their primitive brains were trying to help them deal with the pain in their lives. They were doing the best they could at the time. I don't only see the pain and consequences I experienced; it sucked for all of us. They didn't want to be showing up to their lives and parenthood that way. No one would honestly choose that, but our primitive brains' survival drive and the pull towards more dopamine hits is *strong*!

It was easier to see the intelligence with my parents than it was with my actions. But because I had done that work, it wasn't too much of a leap to extend that grace to myself. With lots of practice.

Instead of hating myself for binging as a kid and young adult, I began to see that I was doing my best to soothe my nervous system/alarm with the easiest things possible: food and sugar. It was actually pretty damn smart! It got the job done very well in the short-term; but there was a lot of suffering that went with constantly using its solution. I started having a little more compassion for my past choices and with that, I was judging myself less, I was forgiving myself. It wasn't a one-and-done kind of thing because it never is. The self-hate and frustration at the weight I'd gained and the food choices I made decreased over time and now they barely make a noise.

I have so much more compassion for myself and everyone else I know and see who struggle with dependence and addiction. It's not easy to live without those easy fixes. It's not easy to choose to sit with uncomfortable feelings, have hard conversations, speak up, when there are things to eat, drink, buy, and do 24/7.

We're all doing our best; and that looks different for everyone. It even looks different from day to day for the same person. Whether you're the person who isn't happy with their behaviors or it's someone you care about, I invite you to look at it with the lens of intelligence to see what they're trying to solve for, how they're trying to help you, and what they want you to know.

CHAPTER 17

Let Go of Shame

It can make your face red, palms and pits sweat, and heart race.

You might want to be swallowed up by the earth or crawl under a table with a blanket over your head and a pint of Ben & Jerry's and a big spoon in hand.

Shame is a very heavy load to carry. It weighs you down, stunts your growth, joy, and potential.

It's like thick molasses that covers us and can be hard to wash off especially when we keep it hidden and in the dark. We think doing that protects us and keeps us safe but it actually makes us sick physically, spiritually, and mentally. We also shrink, trying to get small and invisible so no one will see us or what we feel ashamed about.

A few years back, I hired an accountant to help me clean up a minor mess I'd created in my accounting software. That's what happens when you kinda sorta pay attention but not really. Cheryl had questions about the state of my "books" and with each one I tried to answer, I could feel shame coming over me like a coating of molasses. As I was *attempting* to answer each question, my guts were on fire, I wanted said pint of ice cream and large spoon *so* bad, and I wanted to forget all about the mess I made.

Each question was more ammunition for me to beat myself up and feel like crap about the mess I'd made. I was absolutely positive Cheryl was going to think I was the dumbest person ever on the planet and that I wasn't good enough to be running my own business. Those were the crappy frequent flier thoughts running through my mind. And what we think others think about us, are really the thoughts we think about ourselves. Hello projection.

I had been wearing a shawl of shame. It was heavy, constricting, and paralyzing. I wanted to ignore the situation, withdraw, and disappear.

But I didn't this time.

I wasn't going to keep shaming myself. So in a kind and compassionate way and tone, I stood up to the part of me that was shaming me, and said, "That's enough, we aren't doing that anymore. We made a mistake and now we're getting help to clean it up. No need to keep rubbing my face in it." I became a loving witness to myself. A friend instead of a foe.

I chose not to let shame keep me feeling bad about myself, and instead, I made a conscious decision. I decided that each of Cheryl's questions was an opportunity to work through my shame and have my own back. I drew a line in the sand and refused to beat myself up anymore. This time I chose to receive her kind and gracious help, clean up the situation, and move forward. I wasn't going to let the problem go on and continue to feel like shit.

I reminded myself that I'm not bad or wrong. I just made a mistake that's very fixable. It's completely my choice *what I make the mistake mean about me.* And I'm not going to make it mean anything about who I am as a person.

And neither should you. No matter what you've done, said, tried, or messed up. No matter how many times. *You* are not bad or wrong. Even if someone has said otherwise. Those were their thoughts and words, not the truth.

I invite you to come out from under the table and we can finish the Ben & Jerry's together. Especially if it's Phish Food or Coffee Heath Bar Crunch. It's important that we share our "shameful" stuff with someone who's earned the privilege to hear it. That's Brené Brown's brilliant guidance.

The initial process of releasing and letting go of our shameful secret isn't fun and doesn't feel amazing in the moment. But the thing is, we *all* have them, so find your safe someone and let it go. You will feel *so much* lighter, freer, and expansive. I know this from experience and I'm so damn grateful to the people who've been a loving witness to the things I've felt ashamed about. Their compassion and kindness helped me rinse off the thick molasses and let go of what was weighing me down.

CHAPTER 18

See Yourself Through "Heart Eyes"

Did someone stand up for you when you were little and something happened to you?

Was there at least one person who showed up for you?

For a lot of us, the answer to these questions is no.

No one said:

- It sucks that you get teased or beaten up at school. I'm really sorry that's happening and I'm going to try to do something about it.
- I see that your mom is passed out on the couch a lot. That's got to be really scary for you. If you want to, tell me about it.
- I notice how the other girls treat you in the gym locker room. There's nothing wrong with your body even though it looks different from theirs.
- I would get really scared too if my parents yelled and screamed at each other all the time. Your house should be a safe place, and I can tell that it doesn't feel that way.
- It's not ok for someone to speak to you like that and I'm going to say something.

When we don't have anyone saying something to the effect that the situation is bullshit, shame grows. Shame grows because we think, "There must be something wrong with me that this is happening, and it must be ok because no one is acknowledging or stopping it. I guess I'm the problem, I'm broken, and need to be fixed."

Nope, nope, and nope. These are thoughts our young brains come up with because to blame our parents or caregivers would sever our ties with them and because, "If there's really something wrong with them then I'm totally screwed. If there's something wrong with me, I can fix it and I'll be ok."

As one of those kids who didn't have anyone speaking up for them, I see you, I hear you, and I can appreciate the shit you went through. And I have a feeling that the shame you felt has turned inward and taken on your own voice in addition to the voice of someone from your past.

So what's a grown adult supposed to do? It's called unshaming, and I learned about it from David Bedrick and Simone Seol.

Take time to acknowledge what you went through, especially if you haven't done it much before, or if you have a tendency to minimize your experiences. If you say things like, "Other kids/ people had it harder than me, it wasn't that bad, it was decades ago, etc." That's all irrelevant. This isn't a contest and time does not heal all wounds.

I will talk to myself, saying things like, "It really fucking sucked that mom and dad fought all the time and that there was so much yelling. You didn't deserve to grow up feeling unsafe, and if I (your adult self) was there with you then, I'd tell your parents to get their shit together, get help, and start showing up for their daughters because the yelling stops now." That gives a loving witness to the part of me that never had one, and it recognizes what I went through. This is incredibly healing and can help you take your power back from a time when you felt powerless.

Next, I'm paying more attention in present moments, and noticing when someone says something that hurts or bothers me. I'll say to myself or out loud to them, "Ouch, dang, that hurt my feelings." That acknowledges the hurt so it doesn't turn into shame. I'm being a loving witness to and standing up for myself. Then I'll decide if I want to say something more to the other person. It's very uncomfortable for me to say something because I've trained myself, and my brain, to be quiet and "not upset anyone or cause trouble." I'd throw myself under the bus before I'd have a hard conversation.

But that pattern has never served me, and has caused me so much suffering and to gain weight in the past, because I was literally eating my feelings and words. Reversing this is possible. It's a practice, so kitten steps.

- Be honest about your experiences. Even if it's just with yourself. You deserve to have your experiences witnessed. Our bodies remember and store our experiences until we process them and let them go. Do the somatic practices in this book because they will help release stored emotions. They've helped me way more than I could've imagined.
- Say, "Ouch," when you feel hurt by someone else's words/ actions or by mean self-talk. It's really important we talk back to others and ourselves, and not let our mean tapes stay on repeat.
- Practice speaking up for yourself, to yourself and others, in small ways. Allow that muscle to build slowly. No throwing yourself into the deep end of the pool. It's not necessary, it isn't kind, and it will backfire.

I'm doing this in real-time and it feels discombobulating sometimes because it's new and brains don't like new things. But each time I do it, I'm rewiring my brain's old pattern, and showing it that it's safe to do this now. I'm also healing old wounds. It feels like putting a really moisturizing lotion on dry, cracked hands.

CHAPTER 19

Tending to Our Samskaras

When I was five, my parents had an extra-large fight. My dad stormed out of the house and was pacing the yard; I followed him outside because I was scared and didn't know what was going on. My internal alarm was blaring and I was in full fight/ flight mode; a mode I was very familiar with. I was like a herding dog trying to get her pack together again.

He said, "I can't stand this fighting anymore, I'm going to just move to California!" My five-year-old brain and heart freaked out, and sheer panic was shooting through my little body.

I burst into tears and said, "What about me? You're just going to leave me?"

I don't remember what his response was but it doesn't really matter, because the foundational fear of abandonment had already been laid, and this situation was the straw that broke the camel's back.

In *The Untethered Soul*, author Michael Singer talks about the concept of *samskara*. In Buddhism a samskara means formation of an imprint, it's like a scab. So when I had that experience with my dad when I was five, it created an imprint, and had a big impact on me. Singer's book is about discovering yourself by getting out of your head and questioning long-held beliefs that don't serve us.

When anything happened after that initial experience, that activated that particular samskara, the scab was getting rubbed and it hurt like hell. It feels awful when our samskaras get bumped because it brings up old emotional pain and we hate that. We do anything and everything to run away from it including eating, drinking, scrolling, shopping, and working.

Until we decide not to.

When my fear of abandonment gets activated my heart races, my stomach clenches, and I want to pull my body into a teeny, tiny ball and crawl in my closet. Today I know what's happening, so I do my best to sit with it instead of run, because running from it doesn't serve me as an adult, and doesn't help my inner five-year-old feel better.

I practice inviting the feeling in and allow it to wash through me. I will literally imagine a friend showing up at my doorstep and I invite them in for coffee. The alarm/feeling/samskara is a warning that something bad may happen and I need to pay attention to it. If I keep running from it, plugging my ears and closing my eyes, it'll get louder and louder. The old original samskara and my little five-year-old wants to be tended to and cared for. When we combine somatic practices and change our mindset, we're addressing our whole selves and not leaving our brains or bodies out of the equation.

It's not fun work, but it is necessary if I don't want to let the samskara run my life by showing up in co-dependent, people-pleasing, and perfectionistic patterns. The work is really satisfying though. It feels really good to take care of myself in these ways. Practice has shown that when I am willing to sit with whatever comes up, and allow it to move through me, it'll pass.

Science has proven that emotions, which are sensations in our bodies, only last about 90 seconds when we don't resist them. I've become willing to feel an emotion for 90 seconds to help my brain and body process it.

Humaning is hard. We *all* have samskaras from our life's experiences. But we don't have to let them run the show or live in us forever when we tend to them with compassion and kindness.

CHAPTER 20

Befriend Your Inner Children

One of my top five favorite non-fiction books, and one that I suggest to all of my clients, is *No Bad Parts: Healing Trauma and Restoring Wholeness with the Internal Family Systems Model*, by Richard Schwartz, PhD. It takes the concept of "inner child" from an abstract and cheesy idea to a very approachable and effective therapeutic technique.

We've all heard about your "inner child," and the concept used to make me want to throw up in my mouth a little. It felt cheesy, fake, inauthentic, and totally unapproachable. Nothing I was reading or being told to practice about my inner child felt doable, so it just kind of fell by the wayside. It felt important but inaccessible.

Until I learned about the Internal Family Systems Model. Dr. Schwartz talks about our parts, aka inner children. You know when you say, "A part of me wanted to go to the party but another part wanted to stay home and cuddle with the dogs on the couch"? We all have different parts that are created as we're growing up and their job is to protect us. No, we don't all have multiple personality disorder, I did ask my therapist that and she assured me that no, this is totally normal.

We all have parts that want to protect us and keep us safe. Often, when you respond without even thinking about it, that's a protector part stepping up. Our protectors did their best when we were kids growing up, but more often than not their thinking and behavior becomes maladaptive as we get older. Their methods don't serve us as adults, and often get in the way of healthy and interdependent relationships with ourselves and others.

I've gotten to know three of my parts: my five-year-old, my 13-year-old, and my 16-year-old. They each "protect" me against different things and take their jobs very seriously. When I first learned about all these people living inside me, I was first fascinated, and then I was really annoyed by them. I wanted them to chill the hell out and stop creating so much angst and struggle internally and externally.

For example, one of my parts is 16-years-old, and could get very anxious when Sully would come home from having drinks with friends. That part was very used to being on guard and hypervigilant when my dad would come home from the bar because there would be chaos and/or fighting between my parents. That part felt it was her job to protect me against anything that even remotely resembled something scary from my past. It took me a long time to show her that Sully is not my dad, but it's working.

Since learning about them I've been actively building relationships with each one so they can see that there is an adult part who will stand up for them and take care of them. On their own, they don't know that there's a 48-year-old in here, too, until I started to take the time to get to know them, show up for them over and over, and gain their trust. As I've been gaining their trust, they're seeing they don't have to be "on the job" 24/7. They can go play, take a nap, or whatever sounds fun to them.

There's one super important part that we all have; the Self. This is the part of you who is wise, intuitive, kind, your spirit, your soul, your essence, and just freaking amazing. Your younger parts are a little like your primitive brain that's only concerned with keeping you alive, and your Self is your calmer, let's-think-things-through, less impulsive prefrontal cortex.

I've noticed when I'm all up in my head, kind of freaking out about something, one of my younger parts is running the show.

And when I'm more centered, clear-headed, and present in my body, my Self is running the show.

It's been uncomfortable, frustrating, and a fun adventure to get to know my parts, befriend them, and show up for them. It involves a lot of reassurance, practice, and it's worth it. I also take time to intentionally spend time with my younger parts as my Self. This practice has honestly repaired decades-old hurts and traumas.

Since learning about IFS, Internal Family Systems, and my parts, I've "gone back" to my younger parts to help them feel supported and show up for them today, how they wanted to be "shown up for" back then. As my 48-year-old Self, I'll imagine going back to the five-year-old and saying to her what would've felt comforting back then. This really works, I shit you not. It creates like a ripple of healing through time, and comforting my scared five-year-old just feels good and like the right thing to do.

I can tell when one of my younger parts is running the show and when my Self is; it feels very different. Today, when one of my younger parts sounds a siren, I talk to her, listen to what she wants me to know, and remind her sweet little soul that I've got her and she can go play if she wants to.

No Bad Parts and IFS have been big keys to really move me forward. The work isn't easy but it is fun and worth it. My younger parts and Self honor your younger parts and Self.

CHAPTER 21

Accept People as They Are

We all have that person or people in our lives, who we wish would just knock it the hell off, behave better, get their shit together, or just stop annoying us so much.

Things would be so much better if they'd just "X."

When we think and act this way, we're creating a lot of suffering for ourselves for three reasons:

- First, we're giving our power away and letting someone else control how we think, feel, and act.
- Second, our state of mind or happiness is dependent on them changing.
- Third, we cannot control *anything* outside of ourselves and when we try, we're arguing with reality. We will lose that game 100% of the time.

And when we think we can or should be able to change others, we create a boatload of drama and suffering for ourselves.

Let's slow our roll and get a 30,000 foot view.

Whether it's fully sunk in or not, our thoughts and feelings are our responsibility, controlled by us, not circumstances or anyone else.

Circumstances are neutral:

- Your child having a fit in Target sucks, but you get to decide how to react.

- Your boss putting another useless meeting on your calendar sucks, but you get to decide how you're going to show up before, during, and after the meeting.
- Your uncle showing up to your mom's birthday party drunk sucks, but you get to decide if it "ruins" the whole day, if you keep your distance, or if you decide to celebrate her another time without him around.

Life is 50/50 and it's perfectly fine to be upset about the thing. And if it's not the first time it has happened, it's time to apply one of my favorite practices.

I present to you, "of course they did," which I learned from one of my coaches, Victoria Albina.

- Of course your kid is having a fit in Target. You told them they cannot have another toy and kids don't like that.
- Of course your boss put another useless meeting on your calendar, that's what they do sometimes.
- Of course your uncle showed up to the birthday party drunk, he has a problem and hasn't gotten help yet.

The thing I want to stress to you is to not argue with reality. Those things are happening, or have happened, and arguing with reality is completely a losing battle.

One hundred percent of the time.

Is it time to set a boundary? Maybe.

Have a conversation? Maybe.

Not take the kid to Target if possible? Maybe.

You get to decide the next best thing to do. Hoping and praying someone will suddenly be different than who they've shown themselves to be is a recipe for disappointment and disaster.

Become aware of how you're doing this in your life. Where are you super frustrated and annoyed AF at someone or something?

Are you arguing with reality? If so, accept that, and have a compassionate conversation with yourself, that you're going to practice doing that less.

Then decide how you want to show up, and who you want to be instead.

Practicing this will put you back in the driver's seat of your life and help you see your power.

Pinky promise!

CHAPTER 22

Let Go of Over-Functioning

Here it is:

Growing up in a home with alcoholism messed me up. My dad drank to cope with my mom's Huntington's Disease, among other reasons, and my mom drank to cope with her illness and my dad's drinking. They were both in such vicious cycles of trying to numb their problems away; all the while creating more problems for the whole family.

I wanted them to be ok because then I'd be ok. That's how it's supposed to work isn't it?

I checked all the boxes for codependency, people-pleasing, and perfectionism. I had a very anxious attachment style; I was constantly looking outside myself for validation, affirmation, soothing, and to try to get a general feeling of ok-ness.

OK-ness never came because those things don't come from the outside. But when you're a kid, you don't understand that and you look to your parents/caregivers for everything. They're "supposed" to be your source of safety and comfort, but often they're not, for all sorts of reasons.

I was also constantly on high alert for intense arguments, escalating fights, and would troubleshoot how I could diffuse them. My radar was always on and scanning wherever we were: the house, the car, at a restaurant, or with extended family.

I didn't want to have friends over and definitely never sleep over, because they'd learn our family's secrets, they wouldn't want to be my friend, and I would die from embarrassment.

I kept people at arms-length because if they knew the truth, they'd never want to be my friend.

And since no one could be trusted anyway, why bother getting close just to be disappointed. I desperately wanted friends but was too scared to make many of them or let them get close. I was a very lonely kid in my own vicious cycle of wanting closeness, but not wanting to let others get close.

If someone needed help, rescuing, or if something needed to be fixed or taken care of, I'd be there faster than the speed of light. Over-functioning was a learned trauma response. It was automatic and subconscious.

It was like I was having an out-of-body experience and would almost be obsessed with helping them. Trying to fix or save was my thing; it made me feel good and more in control of my life. It became the most important thing. It's also where my self-worth came from. I thought, "maybe if I helped this person they would give me the attention and love I craved so badly!"

All the behaviors I learned as a kid growing up in a dysfunctional home became automatic habits, like breathing, blinking, and my heart beating. These behaviors were wired into my brain, especially since those childhood habits took root when my brain was still developing. They were as deep as a dandelion's root. Have you ever tried to pull one of those suckers out? They are long and thick!

So how do you change this habituated behavior?

- First, you need to become aware of what you're doing; become like a detective or scientist collecting facts and data without emotion and judgment. You can't change something that you don't see.
- Next, notice your patterns and what you're trying to achieve by doing the thing. Are you trying to change

someone so they change behavior that's upsetting you? Your focus becomes getting them to change so you feel better, instead of taking care of yourself regardless of their behavior. You need to stay focused on you instead of focusing on them.

- Then you need to bring your body back into the picture with somatic practices. The practices combined with a little more self-compassion which is tough for all of us at first because we're so used to beating ourselves up. It's really easy to be like, "WTF am I doing? What's wrong with me that I keep attracting the same kind of people/relationships into my life?"

It's important to be one percent more compassionate to yourself. You were doing what a child thought was best and it got you here, yay! Our inner children/alarms only wanted to keep you safe and alive and now you get to decide if you want to keep, or tweak, their patterns. If you grew up in a home with dysfunction and chaos, unhealthy habits are the norm. You didn't know better and you did your bestest. You wanted to fix things so everyone could feel better, be happy, and make the suffering go away. It wasn't our job but we took it on anyway.

Now you're probably realizing you want to do some things differently, so try to not shame or beat yourself up for old ways of coping. I continue to practice this when my brain wants to beat me up. You were acting from a trauma response. Please be kinder and gentler to yourself. Like you would to a puppy or kitten that doesn't know any better and are looking to you for guidance and love.

It's really important that you to come to terms with a few truth bombs:

- You can't change anyone else. Only you. Period. End of story. Nothing you say, do, beg or plead will get them to change. This takes a hot minute to truly and fully sink in.
- As important as it is to realize you can't change anyone else, it is even more important to see that it's *not* your responsibility to change or fix anyone else. (If it's your child under the age of 18, that's a different conversation.)
- They are not your responsibility.

Accepting these truth bombs was like trying to swallow a boulder. It took me a long time to wrap my head around them because I felt like *everything* was my responsibility. It was like someone was telling me that gravity doesn't work anymore. It did not compute and took a lot of painful trial and error to sink in. I thought it would all be ok if I just tried a *little harder.*

It felt totally unnatural and wrong to just let someone be. Let them be in their dysfunction, deal with consequences of their actions, and not try to fix them. It felt *so* uncomfortable, like I was going to burst out of my skin if I didn't do something. But letting go gets easier and easier with practice.

Supporting someone in their recovery is very different than trying to fix them. They have to want it. They have to put in more effort, energy, and work than you are. It may even feel like you're being a "bad" friend, spouse, or parent. You're NOT. It's their responsibility, not yours.

Please give yourself compassion. Keep forgiving yourself for your behavior in the situation. You were doing your best and what was natural to you at the time. What you thought was the best thing for them and you. Take time to look at why you're in this pattern. Practice sitting in the discomfort of not rescuing or trying to fix them and take kitten steps to live your beautiful life.

CHAPTER 23

Bilateral Activation

We believe we can think ourselves out of our emotions, completely ignoring and forgetting a stellar tool, our bodies. I know that was my M.O. for decades. But it's time to slowly and compassionately bring our sweet bodies back into the equation because they're a part of the solution.

When we experience alarm, anxious thoughts, or other big emotions, the whole brain is involved but it tends to be more activated on one side a little more than the other. What we're going to do in this chapter is disrupt anxiety's signal so it can't keep its act together and we can respond from a calmer state.

- Start by drawing an imaginary line down the middle of your body, that's your midline.
- Take anything small that will be easy to pass from one hand to the other. Put the thing in one hand, and pass it in front of you, crossing your midline, and place it in the other hand.
- Then take that hand and pass the object back across your midline placing it in the opposite hand.
- You're passing the object back and forth from one hand to the other, crossing the imaginary line down your middle each time. It can feel weird, awkward, and a little hard to do in the beginning. That's ok, keep at it.

You're going to notice quickly that your level of anxiety has gone down because our brains can't stay at a high level of anxiety when we're engaging both hemispheres. You're disrupting the neural pathways that the big emotion was on. It's like when you see someone spin around and then try to walk in a straight line; you're making the big emotion dizzy so it can't keep you on the activated pathway. Then you can respond from your non-activated prefrontal cortex.

You can do this anywhere with anything:

- Your water bottle
- Earbuds case
- A pen
- Your phone
- Anything smallish and handy

Kids can do this under their desk at school. You can do this during meetings or subtly at social gatherings without anyone knowing that you're calming your alarm and soothing yourself. Practice this throughout your day, not only when you're experiencing a big emotion. Allow it to become a routine, normal part of your day like brushing your teeth, drinking water, or peeing.

This will create a helpful default pattern in your brain, one you can pull out of your toolbox anytime you want.

CHAPTER 24

Why I Cut Out Sugar

To say I've had a complicated relationship with food, especially processed sugar, is as big an understatement as saying the Grand Canyon is a little hole. I started eating to soothe myself when I was ten and quickly became a binge eater.

I became a stealthy ninja, sneaking treats, rearranging cookies in their container so it wasn't super obvious that I took a bunch, taking money from my mom's purse (she said it was ok, but still) to buy things, stuffing my stomach way past the point of discomfort, buying things in my high school's store or vending machine and eating them in secret in a bathroom stall, and going through various drive-thrus and binging in my car.

One year ago, I drew a line in the sand because I was tired physically, mentally, and spiritually of living a life that was just "fine." Way more than fine in countless first-world ways, but also not fine, because I knew I was cutting myself off at the knees.

I had my spark, shine, effervescence, but they could only shine so bright because I was dulling it with sweets. I was eating little cups of milk chocolate chips, no dark chocolate please, or ice cream most nights. You might say, "What's wrong with that? Everything in moderation."

I've learned that sugar, not the amount of sugar found in ketchup and dressings, doesn't feel good in my body or mind when I eat it regularly. Believe me, I tried. Many, many, many, many times.

And a few more times *just* to be sure.

If I had chocolate chips in the pantry or ice cream in the freezer, it was going to wind up in my belly very soon. I'd eventually wave the white flag and give in after *a lot* of mental tug of war and white knuckling, so the voice in my head would just STFU already. I later learned that voice was due to wonky dopamine levels and there was something I could do to "unwonkify" them.

It totally felt like sugar, not me, was driving my bus and I hated feeling controlled by sugar. I was sugar's bitch at night after dinner. I had no desire for it during the day and never wanted anything from the small bucket of candy in our pantry. But after dinner I would have such a strong craving. Fighting the craving was almost physically painful because at the most basic level, physical and emotional pain run on similar neurological paths in the brain.

I want to feel in control of my life, as much as one can in a healthy way. So after *a lot* of back-and-forth, and a final come-to-Jesus convo with myself, I decided it was time to try another way. Because for the love of all things good and holy, there *had* to be a better way to live!

I told my wife I was not going to eat chocolate, ice cream, cookies, cake, etc. for 30 days and see what happened. I chose 30 days because Dr. Anna Lembke, author of *Dopamine Nation: Finding Balance in the Age of Indulgence,* shares that that was the amount of time she suggests her patients stop doing the thing they wanted to quit, to allow their body's dopamine levels to reset.

When we keep giving into, and doing the thing, it jacks with our dopamine levels and keeps us in an unhealthy cycle. That could be eating sugar, drinking alcohol, scrolling on your phone, looking at porn, or shopping online.

According to a Harvard Health Publishing, Harvard Medical School, article published 7/20/21, "Dopamine is most notably involved in helping us feel pleasure as part of the brain's reward system. Sex, shopping, smelling cookies baking in the oven - all these things can trigger dopamine release or a 'dopamine rush.' This feel-good neurotransmitter is also involved in reinforcement. That's why, once we try one of those cookies or glass of wine, we might come back for another one, two, or three. The darker side of dopamine is the intense feeling of reward people feel when they take drugs...which can lead to addiction."

Dopamine also plays a role in these functions:

- learning and attention
- mood
- movement
- heart rate
- kidney function
- blood vessel function
- sleep
- pain processing (physical and emotional)
- lactation

Dr. Lembke's book is fascinating and explains so much about human behavior and why we do what we do. Especially when it comes to things we are "addicted" to or crave.

One of my biggest takeaways from Dr. Lembke's book was that my brain was behaving *exactly* how a brain is supposed to when we eat sugar. I wasn't weak, broken, screwed up, morally deficient, or doing something wrong. My brain and body were responding exactly as they were designed to.

I cannot overstate the amount of relief I felt when I learned that. I was like, "Huh, so nothing's wrong with me and this is exactly how I'm supposed to respond? I'm supposed to want more cookies, chocolate, and ice cream. I'm supposed to want more the next night when I'm tired and don't want to feel a feeling. There's nothing wrong with me that I want more?!" You could've knocked me over with a feather!

Let me be clear, I was terrified of going 30 days without sugar. I'd gone ten days before, which was so-so. My brain was convinced that I would die a painful death if I tried; like someone was taking away my beloved stuffed animal or security blanket, because that's what those things had become. I felt scared, uncomfortable, and like someone was taking me out to the middle of the ocean to throw me in and wish me the best of luck without so much as a door to float on.

The first few days I was pumped and happy with myself for making the decision. After two days, I was shocked at how much better I felt physically. No mental fog, no morning lethargy, I woke up rested before my alarm (seriously WTAF is that awesomeness?!), no beating myself up for doing the thing I said I wasn't going to do, my self-esteem was growing because I was following through on something important to me, and I had way fewer anxious thoughts.

In order to complete the 30 days, I had to be willing to get more comfortable with the discomfort of a little boredom, feelings I'd previously pushed down with food, asking for help more often instead of trying to do all the things myself, speaking my mind more, to name a few. I'm having more fun without sugar needing to be a part of the experience. Watching TV at night, or a movie on the weekend, usually meant a chocolate snack. It doesn't now.

I'm discovering all the emotional reasons I was reaching for, and eating sugar. Reasons like boredom, not wanting to speak up or have hard conversations, and shame.

So much shame. Metric tons of shame. I ate because of shame, and I was ashamed of how and what I ate. It was a vicious cycle that I could not figure out how the hell to break.

I felt shame about:

- My body, what it looked like, how it moved.
- My weight, the stupid fucking BMI number and the numbers on the scale–I was *positive* that everything would be fine if I reach my "goal weight."
- What I ate, how much I ate, why I ate.
- The rolls of fat by my bra or top of my jeans.
- Things I've done to try to get attention and affection.
- Things I did as a kid that I'm still unpacking.
- Not speaking up for myself.
- Throwing myself under the bus.
- Holding myself back.
- Sitting on the sidelines and not going for all the things I wanted.
- Shame for growing up in an alcoholic home and *all the things* that come with it.

I'm learning who I am without the crap that comes with hiding behind sugar, numbing myself out, and having jacked up dopamine levels. I had no idea what was just out of arm's reach. I thought it was *adding* fun, joy, and rewards. But it was actually costing me my authenticity, self-esteem, confidence, and sky-rocketing my alarm and anxious thoughts.

My brain had me convinced that going without processed sugar was going to be pure hell on earth. The thoughts I had about the 30 days, and what that would be like, were a gazillion times worse than the actual experience of the 30 days. Which is usually how it goes because our brains turn up the drama and spin all sorts of stories to keep you from taking away their dopamine rushes, normal routines, and trying something new. There were moments of discomfort, but *nothing* that compared to the daily beatdowns and shame I was feeling about how I was living.

Going 30 days without cookies, chocolate, and ice cream changed my life:

- I don't feel like sugar or cravings for it are running my life anymore. I have no desire or craving for sugar. I. Never. Thought. I. Would. Ever. Experience. That. I *never* turned down something sweet.
- I'm not constantly thinking about if, or when, I'm going to have chocolate that night. That alone freed up so much time, energy, and angst.
- The shame has gone way down because I'm not compounding it on a daily basis. Which gives me an opportunity to work though the other situations and experiences that were activating shame for me.
- My self-esteem has gone up because I'm not slowly chipping away at my integrity by constantly going back on my word about eating sugar.
- I'm more confident because I did something that scared the fuck out of me and bonus, I didn't die like my brain told me I would if I did this huge new thing.
- My relationships have improved because I've gotten better at having hard conversations, setting and sticking to boundaries, I'm not in a pissy mood because I'm mad at myself for eating sugar and feel sluggish, and I'm seeking out more opportunities to have fun.
- I don't feel like shit about myself so saying, "no" is getting easier without worrying about the other person's reaction.
- My body is finding its natural weight because I'm not eating a bunch of empty calories and retaining water due to the extra carbs. I am not anti-carb! I'm very pro-carb in fact!
- My self-reliance and capacity to deal with hard things is growing.

- My internal alarm and anxious thoughts have decreased because I'm not having sugar highs and crashes.
- My joints aren't stiff and sore from the inflammation that sugar causes.

I've had a couple DQ Blizzards and a few other sugary things since June and they haven't sent me back to the sugar spiral I was in before. But I do get a headache, I feel more alarm, and I can feel the cravings sneaking back in ever so quietly. Eating processed sugar isn't worth it for me. I sure do enjoy the crap out of the Blizzard for the 20 minutes I'm eating it, but I might "pay for it" after. The price is too high anymore. The return on investment is in the crapper.

Sometimes I have FOMO, fear of missing out, but it doesn't last long when I remind myself of why I'm going to pass on the thing. I'm trying to have my back as much as possible.

There's been a part of me that's been afraid to fully live out loud: because of patriarchy, how we're socialized in the U.S., something my sister said to me when I was 17 that cut deep, and not wanting to put myself out there too much in case I developed Huntington's Disease which I had a 50-50 chance of developing. My brain's logic was if you don't live or love fully, you'll lose less if you get sick. This is what it looks like when we let our primitive brain make our decisions and run the show. I tested negative for the gene in 2007, praise all the things!

Sugar was an easy way to try to soothe my alarm, uncomfortable feelings, and keep me operating at half speed but it was a lose-lose plan. I'm doing the work with my life coaches and therapist because it takes a village. The work is worth it because I believe all of us are here to thrive and not just survive.

I used to think hiding and numbing out behind sugar was the "easy way out." But it was actually a miserable way to live.

I felt like shit about myself a good 60% of the time. That was a really hard way to live that rippled into every area of my life, without exception.

I'm so fucking grateful that I took the chance and believed what my heart and gut were telling me. There is so much wisdom inside us but we've been trained to stop listening to it. The more I get back to listening to the quiet inner whispers of guidance and direction, the more I thrive.

CHAPTER 25

Trust Your Body's Signals

We all have times when our brains are extra active. They go into overdrive problem-solving mode and can drive us bananas. We feel like we're on a merry-go-round or hamster wheel, spinning and spinning. We've forgotten that there's a body attached to our brain. But when we slow our roll just a bit and drop down into our bodies, we can give ourselves the opportunity to reconnect with ourselves, quieting our brains and soothing our alarm and nervous system.

If you were socialized as a woman, you heard subtle and not so subtle messages that you can't trust your body.

- We were taught that super skinny is the only acceptable body size and so we deny our feelings of hunger and fullness.
- We choose a salad when we want the nachos.
- When we were kids we were taught to give adults hugs when we didn't want to, and to allow people to touch us in ways that didn't feel right.
- We stifled our body's "no's!"

We're taught we're not ok as we are, so why the hell would we trust this thing that is "inherently" screwed up and wrong?

I have two office spaces: a home office for my coaching calls, and a suite I share with my good friend Gina, where I practice massage therapy and bodywork. A mutual friend was looking for space to see her clients and Gina asked if I would mind if she used our office on Sundays since neither of us are there.

My first instinct was to say no, that doesn't feel right, but I overrode that feeling because I wanted to help a friend. But as Gina and I were talking about how much to charge her, I kept getting stuck. I wanted to come up with a number that felt fair to all of us, but something kept getting stuck in my craw. I was getting agitated on a level that didn't fit the situation. Over time and with awareness, I've learned that agitation is one of my signals that something's off. It's one of my "check engine lights."

My brain kept telling me to, "Be nice, we can make it work, you're not there on Sundays, who cares if she and her clients are there, don't be selfish." This is exactly what toxic socialization and internalized patriarchy sound like! I felt like I was bullying myself, pushing, and forcing an outcome because I didn't want to change my mind when I already said yes. That wouldn't be very nice, and we all know that being nice is the most important thing if you're a girl.

The next morning, after my wife left for work, I poured myself a big mug of decaf and sat quietly for a few minutes. The still and gentle voice from my body and gut was there saying, "Please listen to me. I don't have an explanation for why, but your answer needs to be a kind no." Once I listened, and gave myself permission to change my mind and honor what I was feeling, I felt a weight lift out of my gut. I could take a deep breath again.

My body felt heard, paid attention to, not dismissed because I didn't have a "good" reason and didn't want to upset anyone. I was experiencing implicit memory, a memory stored in the body that doesn't have a direct situation tied to it that you remember. It's where you don't have to consciously work to remember it. Like reading this, you don't have to remember how to read; it's automatic.

I did feel a little discomfort telling Gina and our friend it wasn't going to work for me. But that small amount of discomfort is nothing compared to the truckload of weight I would've felt had I thrown myself under the bus and bullied myself into something that *didn't feel right.*

I'm learning I don't have to offer a big explanation, or any for that matter. I just need to listen to the messages my body is telling me and be brave enough to honor them as often as possible, giving myself grace and compassion when I need to change my mind.

For most of us, making friends as an adult is uncomfortable and clunky. It's going to feel that way if/when you decide to repair your relationship with your body and make friends with it. You've been talking shit to it for as long as you can remember. We've all done it and your body will forgive you. It's not thinking twice about it, so there's no need for you to either.

Let's skip the judgment and added layers of shame and move forward. You can decide that enough is enough and you're done. Keep reminding yourself this anytime your brain slips back into old habits. No problem, just shift your focus. You're rewiring your brain. It doesn't happen overnight but it does happen quickly with practice.

We *can* be friends with ourselves and trust our bodies and intuition again. We don't have to ignore or be at war with ourselves. We can come back home to our bodies and spend a little more time there instead of living 24/7 in our noggins, our melons, our think machines. We can practice listening to ourselves, honoring what we hear, and soothing and comforting ourselves more often.

Kitten steps, that's all, little kitten steps.

CHAPTER 26

Fear or Intuition?

Is this fear or my intuition?

That is such a good question that I've asked myself and get asked by my coaching clients. It used to be very hard to tell the difference between fear or intuition, and I often mistook one for the other. It took practicing awareness of my thoughts, and attention to what was going on in my body, to start to be able to differentiate them.

Once you start checking in with your thoughts and body you'll notice they have very different energies, volumes, and levels of patience. Literally ask your brain and body, "Is this fear or intuition?" and it will begin to answer you.

This is how I notice and experience fear in my body:

- Like a fast zippy energy.
- Lots of "urgent" thoughts!
- Like I just chugged a large Diet Coke from McDonald's. They have the best soda don't they?!
- My body wants me to *keep moving* to get out of danger.
- It's loud and tells me I have to do the thing *now!*
- My internal "check engine light" appears.
- My blood pressure goes up.
- My chest feels tingly.
- I breathe very shallowly.
- I have a hard time relaxing or sitting still and feel tension in my jaw, neck, and shoulders.
- My digestion will slow down or stop. Hello constipation.

Think of fear like a flagger at an airport bringing a plane to the passenger boarding bridge. Said flagger has had *a lot* of Red Bull, has orange flags/wands, and a yellow vest. Their arms and flags are flailing all over the place trying to get the pilot's attention. Because your primitive brain is only concerned about your safety, it sends your body the physical sensations of fear (flags/wands) to get your attention so you can assess the situation and determine if you need to act. It's normal, natural, as it should be, and nothing's gone wrong. Fear is the airport flagger and it's how your brain gets your body's attention to help you determine if you need to fight, flee, or chill. Fear is your body trying to get your brain's attention so you can decide how to respond.

On the other hand, when I'm noticing and experiencing intuition in my body:

- The energy is present and steady, and not chaotic and life-or-death.
- I can take deep breaths and long exhales.
- My blood pressure is normal.
- Seemingly serendipitous experiences happen.
- I'm able to look at multiple things instead of being hyper focused.
- I feel a calm peaceful wisdom deep in my belly.
- My digestion is normal. Buh-bye constipation.
- I'll have vivid dreams that offer tools and solutions to what's on my mind.
- I sleep well instead of waking up multiple times worrying.

Intuition is just as audible when I'm willing to be present and listen. It's encouraging, gentle, calmer, and inviting. It has a peace and wisdom to it. It doesn't have any flags and it's been sipping chamomile tea in a comfy leather chair in front of a beautiful fireplace.

Fear and intuition are very important for our health, happiness, and survival. We don't need to try to get rid of fear. It's like when the smoke detector goes off at my house. Is it going off because the house is on fire or because I've burnt toast? Do I need to call the fire department or open a window? Notice and acknowledge the message that your brain is sending you, thank it for its warning and for only wanting you to be safe, and then decide what to do next. Nothing has gone wrong. This is how all eight billion people on the planet are wired.

You can start to distinguish between fear and intuition by:

- Put one hand on your belly and one on your heart.
- Take three deep breaths with looooong exhales.
- Notice the sensations in your body, are they fast and urgent or slow and knowing?
- Ask your body, "Is this fear or intuition?" and then name it out loud or to yourself, "I'm experiencing fear," or "I'm experiencing intuition."
- If the answer is, "I don't know," encourage your brain and body to take a guess, especially if this is a new practice. You'll get there, Sunshine, just keep at it.

Learning the distinction between fear and intuition is so helpful for making friends with yourself and building your confidence and integrity.

You got this, Sunshine!

CHAPTER 27

Body Neutrality

In 2006 a documentary titled, *The Secret* was released, and it spoke to me down to my bone marrow. I felt like I was finally hearing and seeing things on the big screen that I'd felt in my core but couldn't articulate. The movie's messages were magnetic and energizing, and I felt them viscerally. I went hard head-first into its main message that positive thinking can change your life and that you can create your own luck.

It spoke to the importance of paying attention to our thoughts. That our thoughts really mattered, we needed to be aware of them, and choose them wisely. That what we focused on, and gave our attention to, was going to dictate our experiences in life. Shitty thoughts = shitty life. Positive thoughts = happy life.

It showed us that we have some say and power over what happens in our lives, or at least how we respond to it. We could put our energy into trying to create what we wanted, and if life took a different direction, then we could show up for ourselves in a positive way instead of letting the curveball take us down.

And one of my favorite take-aways: the Universe is on our side and we can co-create with its energy to make some cool shit happen. As a kid who grew up feeling very alone, it was so comforting and empowering to realize the biggest source of love and good juju was actually cheering for me and wanted to help me create a fantastically full and amazing life! Mic drop.

Everything I heard felt like the truthiest truth that was ever truthed. I had a felt sense that said, "This is big, pay attention, and this is important information, don't waste it." It was like a splash of cold water on my face, a wake-up call. It was like being given a coveted golden ticket from *Willy Wonka & the Chocolate Factory*.

With my reignited internal energy, imagine a Labrador Retriever whose owner just came home, I would sit down with my newly-purchased journal and pens and get to work manifesting more money, more massage therapy clients, and a thinner body. I would write things like:

- I now wear size six jeans.
- My body is beautiful and I'm a goddess.
- I've easily reached my goal weight of 135 lbs.
- I can see my collar bones.
- I love salads and healthy foods.
- It's easy and fun to shop for clothes.
- I don't have a muffin top.
- My swimsuit is my friend.

What I didn't know then was that we won't get the results we want if we do a 180-degree pendulum swing with our thoughts. The new, pie-in-the-sky thoughts are too far from where you are now, so your brain will not even remotely believe them. You'll stay exactly where you are now with an extra dose of shame and blame because you, "Must be doing it wrong, and what's wrong with me, and I guess I don't deserve the thing so I'll just quit and accept my miserable life."

When I would write and say my "mantras" my brain was like, "Whatever, you are not a beautiful goddess. Have you looked in a full-length mirror lately?" Yep, brains are assholes sometimes.

I appreciate the awareness *The Secret* brought to the importance of paying attention to our thoughts and energy. Awareness of your thoughts and energy is a very important piece to creating the life you want. And they missed a crucial kitten step that would've really gotten me where I wanted to go, albeit, in a slower and less show kind of way. The crucial kitten step they missed was suggesting some middle ground thoughts. Thoughts between my then-crappy ones and the "rainbow and butterfly" ones I was trying to believe.

The middle ground thoughts I wish I had back then, fall under the concept of body neutrality. A term I first learned from the always awesome, Jonathan Van Ness, JVN. If you don't know who they are, Google them, you're welcome! Body neutrality is the middle ground that was missing from the tools *The Secret* gave us. It's the kitten step instead of the huge and impossible leap. The doable and reachable next thing instead of needing a super tall ladder on your tippy toes only to miss it by ¼ of an inch.

Body neutrality is the ability to accept and respect your body even if it isn't the way you'd prefer it to be, according to a *New York Times* article.

Body neutrality looks and sounds like:

- "I have a body," instead of, "I hate my body," or, "I'm a beautiful goddess!"
- Unfollowing people and pages on social media that emphasize crazy diets and looking a certain way instead of doing what works and feels good to you.
- "My stomach protected growing bebes," instead of, "My stomach should be flat," or, "I love all my stretch marks!"
- Buying comfortable clothes that feel good for the body you have right now and getting rid of your "skinny" jeans or "goal weight" clothes.
- "My legs get me from point A to B," instead of, "Look at that cellulite," or, "Some people don't have the use of their legs, I should be grateful!"
- Getting into the pool with your family instead of hiding

behind your cover-up and taking poolside pics.

Kitten steps, Sunshine, kitten steps.

We have a better chance of getting to the place of loving and appreciating our bodies if we first spend some time in body neutrality. We can't rush to the opposite of what we currently have and expect it to stick because it never does and we've all experienced that spiral of shame.

We can be happier right where we are, when we're willing to believe that "over there" (being thinner) won't be some magical solution to all our problems. That's taken a hot minute to sink in but it has. Join me in the middle ground of accepting our bodies where they are today. You can still make wise changes with what you eat and how you move your body, without berating yourself or dousing yourself with fake positivity.

You got this, Sunshine! Let's go cannonball into the pool together!

CHAPTER 28

Make Peace with Your Body and Your Closet

One of my clients had a bug issue in her home and was having a pest company come out to get rid of the annoying little buggers. She mentioned a few cluttered areas that she needed to tidy up so the technician can spray, and how she could use this as an opportunity to get rid of stuff. She said she decluttered them this past winter, but things got messy again.

I asked if she wanted to get curious about why they got messy again, because we don't judge 'round here, and she said yes. The first category she mentioned is clothes. I asked her to tell me about what's in her closet.

1. She said she has "goal outfits" that she hopes to fit into one day when she's at a different weight.
2. She said she has "hater outfits." Things she wears when she doesn't feel great in her body.
3. She said she also has jeans "that make me sad" because they don't fit her body right, meaning they make her feel bad for having natural curves.

Let's break each one down to see the thoughts and feelings she's having about them and reasons we hold onto them.

1. "Goal outfits"
   - Thoughts/feelings about them: one day I'll be thin enough to fit into them (fantastical thinking), I should

fit into them now (shame), I paid good money for them (guilt), my body isn't ok as it is (rejection).
- Reasons we hold onto them: we think having them will *finally* motivate us to make changes.

2. "Hater outfits"
- Thoughts/feelings: I feel like shit and look like shit and these are the only things that are sort of comfortable (defeated, hopeless, self-loathing, disgusted).
- Reasons we hold onto them: to shame ourselves for the chips and queso we ate last night, and to try to force change.

3. "Clothes that make me sad"
- Thoughts/feelings: my body is just wrong and it shouldn't look this way, I shouldn't have hips, thighs, or a stomach (shame).
- Reasons we hold onto them: to remind ourselves that it's our bodies that are wrong and we need to *keep trying* to fix it until it fits into mass-marketed clothes.

Those three groups of clothes are keeping her in a shitty place mentally and not serving her. The common thread between the groups is not accepting your body where it is, and believing it should be different in order for you to be happy and like yourself (and using shame to try and change our bodies and our habits).

I told her to get rid of them all because there is no helpful or kind reason to keep them. At the end of the day, they bring her down and make her feel like crap.

It's time to stop beating yourself up and waiting for a future date to wear clothes that feel good right now. If your budget is tight or you like to thrift, grab some friends and go thrift together. You don't need to buy a completely new wardrobe, just some good foundational pieces that feel good and you like how they look. You deserve that.

- Do a Google search to learn about local charities that accept clothing and accessories. Your donations will help people take their next kitten steps and you can often get a tax deduction for your donation.
- Have a fun clothes and accessories swap with your gal pals. Make it a girls' night with snacks, beverages, and music. No kids or partners. You'll have new duds and bling, wonderful memories, and all for the price of snacks and bevvies.
- Sell your clothes, shoes, bags, and other accessories to a consignment store. Get some money back and buy things that put a smile on your face.

You can begin to accept where your body is now, and with kindness and compassion, work to change it if you want to. Accepting your body where it is in this moment doesn't mean you resign yourself to your current body for the rest of your life. And it doesn't mean you're going to eat double cheeseburgers and fries with a chocolate shake forever. It means you're calling a truce with yourself, accepting what currently is, and taking kitten steps in the direction you want to go. Both can be true. You can be ok with where your body is now, and work to make changes.

Once you've said, "Buh-bye Felicia," to the clothes that aren't serving you anymore, it may be time to get some that do:

- Swap goal outfits with ones that fit your current body and look great on you. So when you see yourself in the mirror, you're like, "Yep, that looks good!"

- Exchange hater outfits with ones that are comfortable, comforting, and that you love to wear. Think flattering but not frumpy.
- Trade clothes that make you sad for ones that make you smile like my Ms. Pac-Man leggings and tie dye shirts do for me.

Do some of the somatic practices in this book to let go of any yucky energy around your clothes or your past choices. Learn from this experience, let yourself off the hook, and move forward. When your brain wants to circle back to the crappy thoughts, redirect it like when your puppy or toddler are chewing on something they shouldn't.

Over and over. It's a practice, not a one and done.

There's no point in beating yourself up. Has it ever gotten you the result you want? It never has for me and boy oh boy have I tried.

When you let the items go, you free yourself from the *enormous* mental load you're carrying and the subconscious energy you're giving them every single day. We give our belongings so much time and energy, consciously and subconsciously. You won't realize how much they weighed you down until you let them go.

My client is going to feel so much lighter and free when she's done with this. I told her to take a before-and-after and let me know how it goes. Before-and-afters are the best because they remind you of your progress and can be great motivators for a future project or task.

What's weighing you down that needs to go? Sometimes it's our stuff. Other times it's old beliefs and thoughts that are like cinder blocks on our ankles. Often it's both. What is it for you? Start with a small little one, because kitten steps.

You're not broken, damaged, or messed up. You're a normal human with a normal human brain and that can always be tweaked to get you where you want to go.

CHAPTER 29

Complete the Stress Cycle

There are two pieces to a stressful situation. The situation itself and the energy you feel in your body as a response to the situation. Most of us think that when the situation is over, we're done with it; there's nothing more to do. But that's only half of the equation.

A quick definition. Feelings/emotions are chemical sensations in our bodies that only last about 90 seconds when we allow them to run their course. Science has proven this, and our ancestors experienced both halves of the equation naturally. When they would be hunting an animal, or were being hunted, they would be physically exerting the pent-up energy that completed the response to stress.

Depending on what feeling you're having, certain hormones are released into your bloodstream to help you deal with the situation. For example, it could be adrenaline to help you flee from a perceived threat. You've got the threatening situation and the chemical sensation in your body.

Most of us don't know about the second part of a stressful situation and think we're in the clear when it's done. We want to get through it as quickly as possible, whether it's physical or emotional (a critical email from your boss or argument you had with your partner).

We're unaware of the leftover chemicals/hormones and energy in our bodies that also needs to be dealt with. We're not taught this part, and how important it is to work through. We're literally walking around with an accumulation of energy and hormones from past situations; unresolved and unprocessed emotions. No wonder there's road rage, arguments between partners that aren't really about the "laundry" or "dishes in the sink," ulcers, high blood pressure, and people losing their shit. We're pressure cookers that haven't learned how to "let the steam out" in healthy ways.

This can leave you living in a constant state of fight-or-flight, which is exhausting and wreaks havoc on our physical, mental, and spiritual health.

I have two black Labs, littermates, Georgia and Carolina. One fine day I let them out to run around the yard per usual. Except there happened to be a chipmunk in the yard.

I hear them chasing it. I'm trying to get them to come inside, in total vain. I'm screaming like a banshee, (sorry neighbors)! Sully comes out and is trying to figure out what to do and how to help, (thanks babe)!

The little bugger did not get to a safe space in time. It wasn't dead, but its chances of a full recovery looked slim. To add insult to injury, I slipped on our moss-covered deck trying to grab two, 55 pound Labs, landing hard on my ass.

We finally got them inside and I was shaking. I was furious that they wouldn't listen, angry that the little bugger didn't get away safely, upset that it was harmed, and my tailbone was throbbing.

I also had a coaching call in 15 minutes. I was present enough with myself to know that I needed to let the energy of the experience flow through me so it could get out. I went back outside to give myself some physical space to walk it off and let it out. Still shaking, I burst into tears.

I sobbed, ugly cried, and snotted all over myself for the injured chipmunk, for my frustration at my dogs' prey instinct, and that I wasn't able to stop it from happening. After my good ugly cry, I literally felt a physical shift in my body. I felt the energy of the experience actually move through me. I was still upset and worried about the chipmunk, but by letting myself have a few minutes to "breakdown," I allowed my nervous system to take care of me by processing the event's energy, and I was ok-ish after.

We're not taught how to support ourselves when things like this happen, and so when a situation is over, we think we're fine. But we're not fully ok if we don't allow the energy to move through us. That unprocessed energy will stay stored in our bodies until we give it an invitation and opportunity to get out.

Our bodies are so smart and will tell us how to do this if we pay attention. Sometimes I need to cry, shake out my hands, have a solo dance party, or talk it out to someone. These actions help our alarms and nervous systems to complete both pieces of a stressful experience instead of leaving it half-done with us wondering why we feel off and out of sorts.

Dogs are fabulous role models for how to release pent up energy and I know you've seen them do this, even if you didn't know why they were doing it. After they rough house or get their haunches up, they do a full-body shake from nose to tail. They are expelling the excess energy in their nervous system!

Humans walk around with so much stored nervous system energy, it's no wonder we feel so much anxiety and get sick!

Two things to get you started:

- First, become aware of when your internal alarm goes off. You'll want to fight back, run away, or totally shut down and can't think straight.
- Second, check in with your body to see how it would like you to get rid of the energy because it won't go away on its own. Literally ask it, "what do you need to let this go?"

Your body will tell you if you listen. This may feel silly and strange to start–that's normal–but your body will answer you and thank you. We need to slowly work with our bodies instead of only living in our heads. You'll carry less stress, be able to handle life's challenges better, and you'll be more in control of your reactions instead of feeling like you're at the mercy of life's circumstances.

Ok, so what are some fun and effective ways to release the pent up energy?

Do what Taylor Swift suggests in her song, "Shake It Off!"

- Dance party it out.
- Shake your hands like you're flicking off extra water.
- Have a pillow fight.
- Go for a walk.
- Take an exercise class.
- Break some dishes you bought from Goodwill just for this reason.
- Sing in your car, home, or shower at the top of your lungs, cry.
- Think about something funny and laugh your ass off.

Move your body in any way that feels good. There's no wrong way to shake it off! When you're antsy, restless, can't sit still; go shake it off. Your body is telling you there's extra energy that it wants you to release. Listen to it, do something, anything.

Resolving the stressful situation *and* shaking it off will help you complete the stress cycle and not have the residual hormones lingering in your body.

The rest of my day was ok because I wasn't carrying the emotional and physical residue of the experience. We are animals, mammals, and when we forget this and stay in our heads all the time, we miss opportunities to help ourselves heal and thrive.

The chipmunk wasn't in the yard when we checked after my coaching call, so I'm choosing to believe it made its way home to recover.

Decide how you are going to shake it off. Have a few things in mind so you can pull them up when you need them.

You got this, Sunshine, now go have fun with it!

CHAPTER 30

Tapping to Release Emotions

Sometimes when we are experiencing our bodies' alarms or other big emotions, we feel like a pressure cooker whose steam needs to be let out. This is because most of us weren't taught about our alarms, that it's ok to have all of our normal human emotions, or how to express and release them.

I learned the following technique from Melissa Tiers. She's an author and the founder of The Center for Integrative Hypnosis with a private hypnosis practice in New York City. This is an abbreviated version of the Emotional Freedom Technique created by Gary Craig in the 1990s. It's one of my favorite ways to soothe my body's alarm and nervous system; it brings us into our prefrontal cortex where we're better able to make rational decisions. It's a technique to quickly and effectively let your emotional steam out in a healthy way. It works by tapping on the same points used in acupuncture and acupressure therapies. Use it anytime you feel yourself in fight/flight/freeze mode or experiencing a big emotion. It will help calm your nervous system so you can take the next right action.

- Start by bringing to your mind and your body the emotion or situation that's feeling really big and rate its intensity on a scale of 1-10. You don't need to stay there, just for a moment so you can tap into it to help release it. You also don't need to describe it or be able to "put your finger on it." Just tap into it.

- Use two or three fingertips from either hand and tap on the top of your head while saying two or three times, "I release and let it go."
- Then tap the area between your eyebrows and repeat the phrase two to three times.
- Move to the side of your eye, on the bone, repeating the phrase two to three times.
- Then tap just below your eye on the ridge of your eye socket repeating the phrase two to three times.
- Then open your palm and gently pat on the middle of your chest, the area near your heart, repeating the phrase two to three times.
- To finish this round, take one hand and wrap it around your other wrist like you were measuring its circumference, take a deep breath in, and very long exhale out with puckered lips.
- Re-rate the emotion or situation's intensity.

You can do this series one to three times or whatever feels good to you at the moment. This has become one of my favorite ways to calm and soothe my alarm/nervous system; and bring my brain and body to a more neutral state so I can think clearer and help myself make a good next decision. I do it most mornings as a part of my morning routine. Brush my teeth then tap. It's my version of meditation and just *feels really nice* and kind to myself.

This exercise is so simple you can teach it to kids to help them regulate themselves which is something most of us weren't taught when we were young. Practice and play with this technique; you can't break it or do it wrong. Each time you do, it releases the energy of the emotion, rewires your brain to create a new pattern with less intensity, and puts you back in the driver's seat to decide what you'd like to do next. It's a beautiful way to *really* take care of yourself.

You got this, Sunshine!

CHAPTER 31

Begin Anywhere

"I don't know where to begin."

"There's a right way to start."

"I don't wanna screw up and look dumb or fail."

These thoughts will keep you spinning your wheels and afraid to take the first step. The primitive part of your brain is trying to protect you from feeling emotional pain and doing new things because new things take energy you might need to fend off a tiger. So it'll send you messages to keep you from starting. Or derail you a couple weeks into a new habit.

Ever self-sabotage? That's likely what's going on.

And even though you might be unhappy in your current situation, your brain tells you to stay put because it knows you'll stay alive doing things you've done before, and it's not sure about your safety if you try the new thing. Your primitive brain is concerned about your safety, not your happiness. Your happiness doesn't keep you alive and the species procreating.

I suggest you practice talking more compassionately to your sweet brain - just one percent more kindness. Your brain is just scared and is best handled with kindness and care, not bullying or name calling. When it gives you one of those warning thoughts, tell it something like, "I hear you, and thank you for the warning. I'm going to go ahead and make the phone call, try the pottery class, start researching a cross-country RV trip, take the dance lesson, etc."

Acknowledging your primitive brain's messages and alarms helps to turn its volume down and rewires default pathways, which creates new patterns and behaviors. Like when a toddler keeps trying to get their mom's attention and usually quiets down after they're acknowledged.

Next, *begin anywhere!*

Literally.

Take one step.

I don't care what it is, just take it. Newton's first law of motion, roughly paraphrased, teaches us that an object in motion stays in motion unless acted on by another force. Taking one little kitten step will help you take another, and another. It will help you get unstuck. And help you figure out what to do next.

Don't believe your brain when it tells you that you have to know every single step in order to begin, because it's not true. You don't have to have the whole route planned out, just the little bit that's in front of you now, that's all. Like when you're using GPS to navigate. It doesn't show you the whole route, just the next part that you need, and then the next part, etc. You get to your destination by taking it one step at a time.

Take that first step, even if it's the "wrong" step because then you'll have more data and information about what worked, what didn't, and where to go next. It will build momentum, self-confidence, and self-trust.

Begin anywhere! Just start. Even when your primitive brain starts its chatter. You get to choose to listen and stay stuck, or to acknowledge it, and then move forward anyway!

You got this, Sunshine!

CHAPTER 32

How to Change Direction

Ever notice how when you keep thinking about something negative, quickly it's all you can think about, and it seems to grow like you sprinkled some damn Miracle-Gro® on it?

That's because what we give our attention to, and focus on, grows. It's called *confirmation bias.* Our brains look for proof and evidence to back up a thought we already have so we don't waste precious energy thinking about something new because we may need that energy to fight off a sabertooth tiger.

The more you focus on how you haven't lost weight, the more you tend to opt for the hard salami sandwich on white bread with cheddar cheese and butter, with a side of Cheetos, instead of the salad you really love that fuels you with energy. I'm not dogging the sandwich and Cheetos because that just hits the spot sometimes, and we need to listen to our bodies and give them what they need.

The more you focus on how your partner isn't helping around the house, the more resentful you feel, and only see how they aren't doing the things you wish they did, even though you haven't used your words to express your wants or needs.

The more you focus on how the dirty laundry seems to resemble Mt. Everest, the less likely you are to do a load here and there, or teach your kids (if age appropriate) to do their own. BTW, that'll get 'em to stop wearing three outfits in one day right quick.

Sophia Petrillo's character on *The Golden Girls* started most of her awesome stories with, "Picture it, Sicily, 1945..." So picture it, your current city, today, and you're headed out for a road trip. You've got your GPS coordinates entered, snacks, beverages, and things to listen to - and you've peed. Always pee before a road trip.

When you have the map up on your screen, there's an arrow or little car icon showing which way you're headed. It doesn't show what's behind you. It shows you what's coming up, where to turn, any upcoming heavy traffic, or accidents. It doesn't show the intersections you crossed a mile back. It doesn't show you other cities or routes. It doesn't show you the past because it will not help you get where you want to go.

When we frequently or constantly look backwards, it's easy to get stuck and stay there. We focus on the things we did "wrong," wish we would've done differently, and somehow think that focusing on what's already happened will somehow change the future. There's definitely a time and place to look backwards. It's important to know how and why we got to where we are now. This is an important step, and one to never be underestimated, rushed, or minimized. But don't stay there.

Focusing on the past, and what you don't want, will not get you what you do want in the future. It will keep you on the same merry-go-round of same shit, different day, and neither of us want that for you.

It does you no good to keep looking at where you've been, or what you've done in the past because neither helps you get where you want to go. This applies to every situation in our lives and not just when we're using GPS in our cars. When we keep looking backwards, at where we've been long after it serves us, we stay focused on the problems and not the solutions.

I don't care where you are on your "road trip through life." Maybe you just decided, like five minutes ago, to change your relationship to food, alcohol, working out, your partner, your kids, or how you show up for yourself.

Focus on which direction you're headed. Stop looking backwards so much. It'll take a hot minute to retrain your brain away from looking at the past so much, to not beat yourself up over every "mistake." Each time it wants to go down that well-worn path, redirect it, like a puppy or baby that gets ahold of something they shouldn't. You don't have to freak the fuck out, just give them something they *can* have. Do the same with your sweet human brain. Don't freak out on yourself that you went back to a habituated behavior; of course you did, it's a well-worn old pattern. Just notice it and redirect yourself. Nothing is linear and all is not lost.

Our human brains love to stay where they are, even if it doesn't serve us. Familiarity is "safe," "comfortable," and "keeps you alive." It doesn't have to use potential life-saving energy, thinking about, and doing the new thing that it may need to fend off lions, tigers, and bears. Your brain is concerned with your safety, not your happiness. This can sound so bananas, like why the hell is my brain still worried about that today? It's still worrying about that today because of the 650 million years of wiring it has had to get you safely to the present day. It's science.

All of that old wiring is what can keep you dwelling on and grousing about where you've been, how you're not further along, and how it's not fair that you've got some work to do. Your brain wants you to stay where you are because it thinks it's safer to do so. You get to decide whether to continue believing its well-meaning, but unhelpful tactics, or to put yourself back in the drivers' seat and make changes.

Start noticing what's going on in your normal, healthy human brain, *and* make the choice to not stay there. When there's a change you want to make but seem to be "sabotaging" yourself, that's just your brain trying to keep you "safe." You're not unmotivated, lazy, incapable of change, or any of the other bullshit mean things you've said to yourself. It is normal. Your brain is working exactly how it's wired to. There is no problem here. The only problem is when you get hooked on the thought, start judging yourself, and stop trying.

I will literally say to myself, "Uff da, (because I'm from North Dakota and that's what we say) there my brain goes again. It's just trying to keep me safe. Nothing's gone wrong. How do I want to move forward?" This simple acknowledgement and question keeps me from staying stuck.

In your life, thinking about the little car icon or arrow, what direction are you headed? Is it the direction you want to go? If not, no worries at all, Sunshine. We can make adjustments to our path and route at any moment. Our GPS does it when we take a different street. They recalculate. It may be time for your own recalculation.

Keep it simple and take small, kitten steps.

CHAPTER 33

Pivot Your Thinking

Did you see the *Friends* episode where Ross, Chandler, and Rachel are trying to move a couch up the stairs and Ross keeps yelling, "PIVOT, PIVOT, PIVOT!"? If you haven't, do yourself a favor and watch it now. You're welcome! This scene is the only thing I think of when I hear the word pivot.

One particular day, my plan was to clean out the car, pack it for vacation, workout, and work with my coaching clients.

I was sitting in my car in the garage, about to run errands, when I got a call that could've totally thrown a wrench in my day. My brain instantly went, "OMG, I DON'T HAVE TIME, I HAVE SO MANY THINGS TO DO, BUT THIS IS TIME SENSITIVE AND WAITING ISN'T AN OPTION!"

My brain was spinning like a top, I got hyper-focused on the new task, my chest got a little heavy, and I couldn't think straight. I'd gone into fight/flight/freeze. My normal brain was telling me that there was a problem, a threat, and my body was responding normally. It was getting me ready to fight, flee, or freeze, in order to protect me from the threat. Nothing had gone wrong. This response has kept our species alive for hundreds of millions of years. It's science peeps, and we just need to practice working *with* it instead of fighting it or thinking something is wrong with you.

What I know now, is that this is an "invitation" and opportunity to pay attention, and decide how I want to respond. It's a check-engine light, that's all. We're supposed to have a reaction when our brains sense a possible threat, and we get to choose what the reaction is.

So I noticed my "check-engine light," the "THERE'S A PROBLEM AND SOMETHING NEEDS TO BE DONE ABOUT IT RIGHT NOW!" and took three good deep breaths with long, exaggerated exhales. It's the exhales, not the inhales, that slow our heart rates and breathing, where our bodies sense we are actually safe, and we're able to pull ourselves from our primitive brain and into our prefrontal cortex.

Noticing my "check-engine light" and breathing, I was able to recognize that I had two choices. I could freak the fuck out and piss and moan about the new task all day which would only keep me spinning in the problem, or I could figure it out. I decided to figure it out. From my calmer prefrontal cortex, I flipped the "problem" of not having time for the new thing, to a helpful question, "How is it true that I *do* have the time to tend to that task?"

Asking the opposite of what my brain was believing, put it to good use because brains love to solve problems. So I answered that helpful question and was able to see that I actually did have plenty of time to take care of the things I planned for and the one I didn't. In the moments of freak out, I was believing what my brain was telling me, and it was mistaken.

All this isn't to say the answer is always that you do have time and you just need to cram it in. Sometimes you need to delegate a must-do task. But by taking some breaths and re-centering myself, I could look at it clearly, without emotion, and make a rational decision instead of listening to the anxious thoughts and believing them.

I've been in many similar situations since this one, where something unexpected is tossed my way, hello life in general, and I do the same thing.

- Notice my brain's normal response to a possible threat.
- Take three deep breaths with long exaggerated exhales.

- "PIVOT!" to ask myself how the opposite of the "problem" could be true.
- Take a kitten step in the direction of the solution.

It only takes a couple minutes to do these steps and get into a solution-oriented mindset. I ended up having time to write a social media post about this experience and take care of a few other things. Amazing things can happen when we slow down and kindly challenge our thoughts.

Throughout the day my brain wanted to go to the space of, "That extra task sucked and it shouldn't have happened." And I'd kindly come back with something like, "It did happen, we did a great job handling it, and we're moving forward." A simple compassionate redirect.

When you're onto your brain's normal and healthy shenanigans, you can breathe, pivot, and move in the direction of the solution.

You got this, Sunshine, just "PIVOT!"

CHAPTER 34

Let the Good Stuff In

It comes in different forms and is known by different names.

Self-sabotage, success intolerance, joy intolerance, or waiting for the other shoe to drop.

There're the things we do when we start to feel a level of joy or happiness that's more than you're used to. It's out of our normal range. Like when we have blood tests and the results fall in the normal range but it doesn't feel good in our body. When we're out of our normal range we feel uncomfortable in our skins. It feels scratchy and tight and we can feel like an imposter. I've experienced this when I get close to my goal weight, have a success in my business, or feel closer to Sully.

It can be a little too much for our nervous systems. We can feel like we're stretched to the point of snapping. Our nervous systems are challenged when we feel an abundance of "positive" emotions, just like when we feel an abundance of "negative" emotions. Nothing's wrong. This is normal and you know I've got your back.

We want *so much* to be happy and living fab lives, but then when it comes our way, we're quick to turn off the faucet or kink the hose.

What does turning off the faucet and kinking the hose look like?

- You get a job promotion but then pick a fight with your partner.
- You get close to your goal weight and then dive head-first into half-gallon of your fave ice cream.

- You're finally getting along with your mom and then impulsively spend $3,000 on a couch your family doesn't need.
- You're getting more comfortable with your partner and then unconsciously feel the need to create distance.

You're basically cutting yourself off at the knees. Two steps forward and one step back.

We've all heard stories of lottery winners who blow their money in a hot minute, and wind up back where they started. This is part of the reason they wind up that way. It's an uncomfortable level, of a feeling they want *so damn bad*, but haven't expanded their capacity to receive or experience it.

It's like when you first start working out or drinking more water. You start with 15 minutes of walking or whatever your fave activity is because we take kitten steps around here. And you're feeling it in your lungs and legs. You can tell that amount of time and intensity takes you to the edge of your ability. This is good and allows you to slightly stretch your capacity. You shouldn't start with an hour-long intense workout because kicking your ass like that is a great way to ensure that you throw in the towel and never do that again. Totally speaking from experience.

Same thing with drinking more water. If you're not used to drinking more than a glass or two of water a day, it's not in your best interest to overload your body by drinking eight glasses in a day. It's too much. Your body needs time to acclimate and adjust. If you want to up your water intake, drink one more glass of water than you did the day before, working up to an appropriate amount for you. What's that amount? Some say half your body weight in ounces. Others say drink enough water so your pee isn't the same color as Big Bird from *Sesame Street*. This was a necessary tangent because getting adequate hydration is like getting adequate sleep.

When I experience the alarm in my body or anxious thoughts, I'll take a few minutes to ask myself if I'm safe in this very moment, and do the tapping shortcut or some other somatic practice. I'll put a hand on my heart, belly, or leg and say something sweet to myself like I would one of our dogs. This calms my body's alarm and shows my nervous system that I will show up for it when it's trying to get my attention.

The same thing applies when you have a big wave of joy or happiness. Your alarm/nervous system needs time to acclimate to the additional input, like with upping your workouts or water consumption.

It's why I like to start my coaching sessions with celebrations. I have clients name a few things they're jazzed about, no matter how big or small. Tiny kitten steps in one percent increments is all that's needed to change the trajectory of your life. Celebrating ourselves shows our nervous systems that it's safe to accept and receive more good. There'll be less self-sabotage-y and waiting for the other shoe to drop because you're stretching your capacity to allow, and feel, the good stuff.

Start by noticing when you downplay or push away the good stuff. We all do it for a variety of reasons. Those reasons can be

- You were taught it wasn't polite to "show off."
- You believe when you have "more" others have "less." Life isn't a pie. You having more does not mean others have less.
- You don't feel worthy of more of the good stuff because you think that you're not doing enough or aren't enough period.

This will be in hindsight at first because it's been a habit to deflect more of the good so don't expect yourself to make a 180 degree change. Little kitten steps. Maybe someone compliments a fun new sweatshirt you're wearing and you downplay it. If it's someone you know, text them later and say thanks. This begins the rewiring process in your brain, yay you! If it was a stranger, just say thank you to yourself when you realize it, that still totally counts in rewiring your brain.

Put your hand on your heart, leg, or belly, and remind yourself that you're safe in this moment. There are no tigers trying to scratch your face off. It'll feel silly in the beginning, and then it'll start to feel more natural, and then it'll feel really good and self-soothing. Like a very moisturizing lotion on dry, cracked hands.

By becoming aware of your current level and slowly allowing more of the thing in, you're slowly stretching your nervous system's ability and capacity to live a full life. It's like when you slowly stretch dough to make pizza. You can't get all aggressive with it or you'll tear the dough. Go slow and give your nervous system time to adjust. There's no rush. There's no hurry.

This is how we tend to our body's alarm/nervous system and learn to process our feelings instead of running from them, pushing them down, or denying them, whether they're "negative" or "positive."

You do deserve the good, even if you haven't believed that, so take bits of time to practice receiving it. It's worth it and that's why you're here. To experience all the joy and goodness you'll allow yourself. Little tiny kitten steps, Sunshine.

CHAPTER 35

Figure Out What Works for You

"I'm going to get up at 5:30 am every day even though I need toothpicks to keep my eyelids open."

"I just need to focus, keep my ass in the chair, and get to work. What's wrong with me?"

"I'm not hungry for breakfast but I hear it's good for you."

"I'm going to do cardio three days a week even though I hate cardio."

I have said or heard those sentences, or a different version of them, from pretty much everyone I've ever talked to. A few things are at play when we're in that mindset:

- We think we'll feel better if we do those things. We'll suddenly shake off all it means to be a human if we just *do* them and finally *"get our shit together."*
- We believe there's some magical life on the other side of accomplishing them; that's called fantastical thinking and I used to spend LOTS of time and money in that la-la land. Spoiler alert, none of those things will be any kind of a magic solution. I found that realization freeing after I was pissed off about it for a sec. I could stop wasting time, money, and energy looking for something that wasn't going to be found there.
- We think we're supposed to be like all the other eight billion humans on the planet. What works for one will work for me and if it doesn't, then there's something wrong with me and I'm the problem.

I want to offer you another way of thinking and living.

What if it was ok to figure out what works for you and do that? It's both obvious and counterculture.

I know that rubs up against all the co-dependent, people-pleasing, and perfectionistic thinking you've been doing for a hot minute. Your primitive brain may have just said something like, "What the hell are you talking about Jenn? I can't do that! I don't even know where to start and what will 'they' say or think?"

I hear you. I'm navigating these waters too because we were socialized similarly.

I'm practicing listening to what works for my brain and body and saying to each their own in every area of my life.

- I never sat down for a set amount of time each day to write this book. I piecemealed it because I didn't want it to feel like a chore, I wanted the process to be as fun as possible, and I'm so over the idea that there's one way to do something! That doesn't even make sense when you say it out loud. It's absurd and ludicrous.
- Some days I use the elliptical, some days I go for a walk, some I do yoga, others I work in the yard, and some I rest. I ask my body what it wants and then I do it.
- I'm not a breakfast eater. I'm not hungry in the morning and enjoy my big mugs of decaf while I wake up and do my routine. I'm a two-meals-a-day person because that works for me.
- Some mornings I'm awake at 5:30 am when Sully gets up and others I sleep until 8:30 am. I used to think there was something inherently better about getting up early but that thought felt like crap so I've thrown it out the window and get up when my body tells me to.

We've got some things working against us that we need to be aware of like long-time habits, others' expectations, not trusting ourselves, following "the rules," and not wanting to rock the boat.

What's the alternative to not addressing those and slowly taking them apart?

Continue ignoring what your spirit, soul, intuition, body, and brain are telling you?

How does all that feel? Like trying to put a round peg in a square hole.

Put simply, it feels like shit. And it doesn't serve you in the long-run.

Start with awareness. Notice when you're forcing yourself to do something that's not "you." I'm not talking about things like attending a meeting at work that you don't want to. I'm talking about things like forcing yourself to get up at 5:30 am when you are not a morning person.

What feels like "you?"

It's okay if you:

- Work for a while, scroll social media for ten minutes, and then go back to work.
- Open all the windows but stay inside on a nice day instead of doing a bunch of activities outside.
- Read books about spirituality instead of going to church.
- Take a walk instead of doing hard cardio.
- Choose not to enroll your kids in extracurricular activities.
- Dislike in-person networking meetings and find other ways to grow your business.
- Don't watch the news or inundate yourself with all the negativity and instead donate to organizations who are doing work you believe in.

- Love the crap outta your partner but sleep in different bedrooms because you sound like a chainsaw and sleep is everything.
- Don't feel like drinking alcohol anymore.
- Choose to not have kids or get married.
- Take medication for your mental health.
- Decide to not have a relationship with a family member because it's toxic.
- Don't give novel-length explanations for your decisions.
- Want to try a glass blowing or painting class.
- Take a solo trip to the beach, Florence, or Paris.

Practice listening to what your quiet and still voice is trying to tell you, and then make a tiny little change in that direction. Remember, we only take kitten steps around here.

You do you, Sunshine!

CHAPTER 36

You're Not Behind

The mornings I don't get up when Sully does, my brain gives me a hard time and says I'm slacking, wasting time, and running behind even before my feet hit the floor. Thoughts like, "You should've gotten up earlier, you've got so much to do, you'll never catch up, and it would be such a better day if you would've gotten up when you planned to!"

I used to feel *so behind* in this situation, not question that thought and feeling, and let it run around in my head unsupervised. I'd believe it like it was a true statement about me, the day, my career, my choices, and life in general.

Part of the reason we freak out about the idea of being behind is because we're pack animals, and not being solid in a pack used to mean certain death to our ancestors. If you weren't in the pack for some reason, you didn't have the support, community, and numbers needed to fend off threats and sustain life. That is still an active and functioning part of our primitive brain's wiring and DNA. The thoughts and feelings of being behind are natural, normal, and don't have to be seen as a problem. We just need to be aware of the thoughts and feelings, not react from millions of years of evolution, and make decisions that feel good to us.

We also think we're behind because we've been told a bajillion times that a certain car, degree, partner, certificate, house, well-behaved kids or dogs, or job, are what we should have, instead of the pretty awesome life we have now. Examples of how I have, and other people have felt behind:

- I don't get out of bed when Sully does.
- I'm taking an online class and had to miss a weekly call.
- Other parents are throwing elaborate birthday parties but you'd like to keep it simple but still super fun.
- You could take on more projects at work but your current load feels good.
- You're turning 25, 30, 40, 55, or 70 and you don't know what you want to do next with your life.
- Other people in your career have more followers on social media, successful podcasts, and five-figure programs that sell out every time.
- You're renting your home/apartment and everyone else seems to own their space.
- You're not as active as other moms in your kids' classes.
- Last night's dinner crumbs are still on the floor.
- Your kid is a junior in high school and they don't know where they want to go to college or what they want to do for the rest of their lives. (Can we collectively stop doing this to young adults pretty please?!)

You are not behind. That's just a crappy thought we've come to believe and it's changeable!

What's a person to do with a normal brain that was socialized and raised in a society that's all about keeping up and not falling behind?

This gal is talking back to my brain like I would my BFF or a puppy. It goes like this.

I don't get out of bed when my wife does, and my brain starts in with its BS chatter. I'll do two things, the abbreviated tapping technique to diffuse the energy, and talk to my brain to turn down the volume of the crappy message, and boost the volume of the better message. The abbreviated tapping technique, described in chapter 30, will help my body release the energy and emotion that is tied to the message of, "I'm behind!" Our emotions are energy, and we need to release the old energy/emotion in order to replace it with one that feels better.

Then I'll say something like, "Good morning sweet melon and thanks a bunch for the warning that I'm going to get kicked out of the pack or won't see myself as a 'good' person if I sleep a few more minutes. I appreciate you lookin' out for your girl, and I'm not believing that anymore."

The things we hear over and over become our thoughts and then our beliefs. Kindly talking back to your brain lets it know you heard its warning, which will quiet it down. Repeating something soothing to your brain will remind it that you are actually safe and helps it to believe you won't die from not being exactly where your pack is.

Our brains love to complicate things because it gives them problems to try to solve, so do not be fooled by the simplicity of this combo. We're not as complex as we think, and the simplest solutions usually are the best. It really can be this simple, I pinky promise. Everything in life does not need to be hard. Keep it simple, kitten.

This is the simple-in-concept-just-takes-practice part of changing your thoughts and rewiring your sweet, normal human brain. It doesn't take years to tweak this pattern, just awareness of what's going on, reminding your brain that nothing's wrong, and you're safe right where you are.

You got this, Sunshine!

CHAPTER 37

Be a Quitter

"Stand by your man."

"You started this so you're going to finish it."

"You're not a quitter."

"Winners don't quit and quitters don't win."

But really, why?

What's the point?

What do you "win" or gain from staying in something that isn't working, doesn't serve you, and might be harmful to your mental or physical health?

Who's voice are you hearing? It's not yours. Is it a parent, sports coach from when you were younger, teacher, or mentor?

This black-or-white thinking that "you should never quit" is a blanket statement that doesn't serve you.

There's a lot of middle ground that needs to be looked at from all directions.

Have you put your all into a relationship but the other person hasn't and it feels like it's time to end it? It's ok to end it. God knows I stayed way too long in relationships that were long past their expiration date but I thought I should keep trying. If those relationships were milk, they'd have been very curdled and smelly.

Reading a book or watching a show that isn't floating your boat? Put it down, find a new one because there's only a bajillion out there.

Took a job that you thought was going to be the bee's knees but it's more like a circle of hell? Find something else.

You do not need to stay in a place or situation that isn't serving you, or worse, because it's "bad to quit."

That is a bullshit lie if I ever heard one.

You might be thinking, "But Jenn, does that mean I just jump ship every time I don't like something?"

No, it doesn't.

It means think about why you believe you should stick it out.

It means don't keep at the thing because you think you "should" or you're worried about what "they'll" think if you change your mind.

It means listen to your intuition, gut, and heart, because they're giving you messages that you might be overriding.

I'm a quitter because my time and energy are precious and I'm not going to waste them when my intuition, gut, and heart are directing me otherwise.

CHAPTER 38

What Are You Making It Mean?

My friend "Stacy" was venting, her word not mine, that she's so annoyed at her ex's behavior, and it was getting under her skin like a splinter that a tweezer couldn't get out.

He's dating someone new, "Ann," and the woman has been attending family and school events that my friend thinks she shouldn't.

Stacy has all sorts of thoughts and feelings about it, they're making her feel like crap, and she doesn't like how she's showing up in her life.

Overall, Stacy likes Ann, and doesn't have any issues with her being around her children. *But,* Stacy has lots of unchecked stories, opinions, and comparisons going through her mind, that are causing her a lot of suffering. These thoughts are bringing negative emotions, and the negative emotions are the root of her problem–not anything Ann is actually doing.

Thoughts like, "Ann shouldn't come to the kids' birthday parties, teacher conferences, and why the hell are they in matching outfits?!" Stacy is arguing with reality, with what is, and the sooner she can see what's going on, and be honest with herself about this the better.

Maybe she's feeling a little replaced now that her ex is seeing someone. Maybe she feels a little threatened that her sons have another adult woman in their lives. Maybe she wishes she and her ex did mushy things like dress alike when they were together.

Don't let your unexamined thoughts drive your bus because they will jack you up so fast. When Stacy was able to slow down, take a breath and be honest with herself; she could see that she was feeling hurt and vulnerable. She could make different choices to take better care of herself and really address what was going on inside, and not just act out in a way that didn't serve anyone.

This is where Stacy's power lies! *She* gets to decide how she's going to think and feel about the situations. Those thoughts and feelings are going to dictate her actions. She doesn't have to be thrilled or throw a party, but the way she's handling things now is causing lots of optional, totally optional, suffering.

When we begin to take responsibility for how we're showing up, reacting to, and responding to a circumstance, we will begin to take our power and control back. It's really easy and common to blame someone or something for how we're feeling. We're socialized to look outside of ourselves for everything which means we're also going to blame people and things for our circumstances. But that's the lazy thing to do and it keeps us feeling powerless and like a victim longer. Own your thoughts, feelings, and reactions, and your life will change in ways you never imagined.

When you notice you're getting your underwear in a bundle about something, ask, "What am I making it mean?" It's not a given that it means what you think it does. Take any topic and people have all sorts of different perspectives about it. Your thought about it isn't the "truth." It's just your thought and perspective from your whole life's experience.

None of this is to say we shouldn't be upset about the thing, far from it. Anger is important. But a lot of us get our feathers ruffled when they don't need to be. If it's important and serves you to be angry, go for it. The point is to think, feel, and act intentionally, not unconsciously.

Realizing that your thought isn't the "truth" will free you of so much suffering! Combine that with the question, "What am I making it mean?" and you're going to change the trajectory of your life.

CHAPTER 39

Working Toward the Thing You Want

As I mentioned before, our focused attention and energy are like Miracle-Gro®. Whatever we give it to, it'll grow, flourish, and thrive. And when our brains get hooked on something, they're like a dog with a bone; they're not going to let it go unless we give it something else to chew on.

Our lives are affected by situations that none of us can control or change, as much as we want to and try. And boy do we try.

We yell, plead, bribe, pray, bargain, shame, or deny to try to change the situation.

But we can't. It's out of our control, which is the hardest pill for some of us to swallow! But swallow it we must or we'll drive ourselves bananas.

Arguing with reality is a complete waste of your precious time and energy. Getting angry is an important part of dealing with a stressful situation. We don't do it enough because those of us socialized as girls are taught that our anger isn't nice, pretty, or lady-like, and we're told we're too emotional and hysterical. That bullshit can fuck all the way off! Allowing and honoring our big feelings helps us process them instead of shoving them down with chocolate, Chardonnay, or anything else we do to suppress our emotions.

Staying in anger and frustration, and fighting what is instead of allowing reality to ebb and flow, drains your energy and leaves you feeling powerless and like a victim. We stay angry and frustrated to avoid having hard conversations or accepting that some things are just out of our control and doing your best to make the situation suck less until you can change it.

If you continue arguing with reality instead of accepting what is, you will lose 100% of the time. It's like getting pissy at the sun for rising, the waves for crashing, or the trees for budding in the spring. Accepting reality *does not* mean you like it, approve, consent, are ok with it, don't care anymore, or forgive them. It means you're done wasting your energy and time trying to control and force a situation to be different. It means you're done treading water in the problem and you're moving toward the solution, which sometimes is just feeling calmer about the situation. It means you're changing what you can, including your thoughts about the situation, and letting the rest go.

Don't fight *against* something.

Work *toward* the thing you want.

The energy is very different in those two perspectives!

It feels like shit to stay in the problem, it doesn't serve you, and it won't get you closer to what you want. Sometimes the only thing you can strive for is a little more inner peace and calm. When you argue with reality you stay in the problem.

Get into the energy of the solution. Shine your flashlight on what you want to feel or see more of, rather than on what you don't want to feel or see. What you give your focus and attention to grows. Use your energy to get where you want to go and not fuel what you don't want.

Feel your feelings, honor them, and get in the energy of the solutions. It's not one or the other, it's both. Your time and energy are so precious. Use them wisely and with intention.

What you resist, persists.

I believe in you! We got this!

CHAPTER 40

Don't Give Up on Love

Most years, a good friend hosts a super-fun Galloween party, a Halloween party for her gal pals. Her home is always so beautiful and she offers all sorts of yummy nibbles and sips. No detail is too small for her creative eye! While at the party I was catching up with one of my favorite humans and she mentioned she's giving up on finding a partner. She said, "Have you seen who's out there!?"

Because I'm happily married I haven't "seen who's out there," but that's not the point. My heart broke for her because she's one of the best people I know! She's so damn funny, thoughtful, a woman of her word, considerate, and you feel better for having interacted with her.

She's a good egg and the salt of the earth. I want her to find someone to share her awesomeness with if that's what she truly wants. And I think it is. But her thoughts of, "I'm giving up on finding a partner," and, "have you seen who's out there," are going to keep her from doing that.

When you're convinced you can't do something, you're absolutely right. Her primitive brain doesn't want to feel the emotional pain of trying, meeting new people, feeling disappointed, and would rather not even try, than keep going for her goal. But what she isn't seeing is that she's feeling disappointed *now*! If she doesn't want to look for Ms. Right because she doesn't want to feel disappointed, too late! She's there *right now!*

Why the hell not keep going? She's letting a feeling she *might* experience in the future keep her from going for it. And she's feeling the feeling she's trying to avoid *now!* Do you see what's going on in her brain? Her normal, healthy brain is trying to keep her from feeling emotional pain in the future. The primitive part of her brain is running the show right now, and it can't see and frankly doesn't care that it's currently creating exactly what she doesn't want.

You're not saving yourself emotional pain by not going for the thing you want. You're creating emotional pain in the moment by keeping yourself stuck, but because your brain is comfortable with what it knows, even when it's pain, it wants you to stay where you're at and not go for the unknown.

If she wants love in her life, she needs to keep going until she has it. Period.

The only reason she isn't is because she believes thought errors like:

- "It'll take too long." What's too long when we're talking about love?!
- "I'll never find someone." Nope, not when you keep repeating crappy and unhelpful thoughts like, "I'll never find someone."
- "Have you seen who's out there?" It's slim pickins when you think there's slim pickins.

I want her to have a great relationship if that's what she truly wants. And if she's willing to be a little uncomfortable, tweak her thoughts, and keep going, she'll get there!

Don't give up on the thing because of crappy thoughts you're believing! Instead, move the old yucky emotional energy through with somatic practices, make little tweaks to your thoughts, and practice the hell out of them.

- "Love is worth waiting for. I've waited this long. I'm just going to keep livin' my life and love will arrive in good timing."
- "There are eight billion people on the planet, there have got to be some good matches out there for me."
- "My friends have found love and it's possible I can too."

Take your crappy thoughts and zhush them just a little, so your brain can believe them, not 180 degrees. You're going for a thought that's a little less shitty than the original. Your brain has to be able to buy into it a smidge in order for it to be helpful.

When you keep practicing your "less shitty thoughts," you're going to find yourself doing things a little differently, being more open to opportunities, and you're going to feel differently. It's kinda magical. Be open to it. You're worth it. Whether it's love you want or something else.

CHAPTER 41

Stop Saying "At Least"

As I write this, it's spring in Indianapolis, and we've had a lot of rain. I posted on social media that I was fucking over it. I was just done, frustrated, and annoyed by the precipitation and everything in my soul was craving the sun and its warmth.

Loads of other people were feeling it too.

And then someone gave me an, "at least…"

"At least it's not snowing."

Are you fucking kidding me with that?

Just, no.

When we "at least" someone we're minimizing and invalidating their feelings and experiences. We're unknowingly saying, "I'm not comfortable with my emotions, so I need you to feel differently, so I can feel better." We do it unconsciously and it can sound like:

- Stop feeling that way.
- It isn't so bad, get over it.
- You should be happy with what you have. Don't be greedy.
- Other people have it so much worse than you. Why are you even thinking about this?

Distilled down, we're saying:

- "I don't know how to deal with my anxiety so I need you to not be anxious."

- "Death is super uncomfortable for me so I'm going to go to the funeral but not talk to my friend because I don't know what to say."
- "You have a job that pays the bills and has benefits, why would you want to give that up to chase a dream?" All the while thinking, "I've given up on my dream, and it hurts to see someone go for theirs because I'll feel like a failure."
- "Why are we thinking about remodeling our kitchen when there are people living in bomb shelters?" (Women are socialized to be selfless and made to feel guilty for having more when others are in need. Life isn't pie. When you have some, that doesn't mean that others have less.)

Stoooop "at least-ing."

"At leasts" are manifestations of our internal "check engine lights." They're alerting us that something is off and needs our attention. Start to notice when "at least" shows up in your life and literally ask them what they want you to know. Get quiet, close your eyes, put one hand on your belly and one on your heart, and talk to them with as much curiosity, kindness, and compassion as possible. They will tell you if you listen.

When we see someone experiencing something and we feel uncomfortable, we want to shut it down ASAP because it reminds us of our unresolved emotions. If we're denying our wants and needs and we see someone going for it, we want to shut that shit down or we'll feel bad for not going for it ourselves.

We all have permission to be annoyed, have dreams and goals, feel angry, create the kitchen we've always wanted, be sad, or shoot for the stars. Feelings, wants, and experiences are valid; no one has the right to minimize or invalidate them, or make comparisons. Wanting and having things does not take them away from others; there's plenty to go around.

Notice when your check engine light of "at least" appears, talk to your "at leasts" with curiosity, and take a kitten step in that direction.

CHAPTER 42

Say This Instead of "I Don't Know"

We believe pretty much everything our brains tell us without question. And our brains will listen to what we tell them when we make small believable tweaks. Kitten steps.

Start by becoming aware of what you're thinking and saying, especially the ones I call our "frequent fliers." Those are the ones on repeat and often aren't even our voices doing the talking.

One of the best changes you can make is tweaking the super-unhelpful-sounds-innocent-and-true, but only-keeps-you-stuck phrase, "I don't know." I'm not talking about the very valid, "I don't know, let me look into it and get back to you," reply that's a good response in many situations.

I'm talking about when something has you spinning, or scared, and your brain just wants to roll around in it like my dog when she finds deer or coyote poop. You just keep telling yourself, "I don't know what to do about it," over and over and over. And you keep telling anyone who'll listen.

Guess what's going to happen when, "I don't know" is on repeat? You'll keep getting more of the "not knowing" every time you repeat that phrase, in part, because brains find it efficient to be "right" so they'll keep you "not knowing" so you're right and don't waste precious tiger-fending-off-energy finding a solution.

Be on to your brain's shenanigans! We can't leave our brains totally unsupervised anymore than you'd leave a toddler or puppy unsupervised. Those are disasters waiting to happen.

This loop-dee-loo is one of your brain's ways of keeping you in the "safety" of the same old same old. It keeps you from taking a small kitten step towards your dreams, goals, better life, less stress, etc. New things are scary to your primitive brain because they don't have a frame of reference for the new thing and so it thinks it could kill you. It will do everything in its power to keep you right where you are, even if it's unhealthy. This is one reason we self-sabotage. It's a safety mechanism from your sweet brain.

A much better option is to tell yourself, and anyone else, "I'm figuring it out." This phrase is empowering, not victim-y, and keeps you moving forward instead of treading water.

- Not sure which school to send your kiddos? You're figuring it out.
- Not sure about that job opportunity? You're figuring it out.
- Not sure how to create a better relationship with yourself, kids, or partner? You're figuring it out.
- Not sure how to start a podcast, create a website, or change careers? You're figuring it out.

Let's play for a second. Say the phrase, "I don't know," and notice how your body feels when you do.

Now say, "I'm figuring it out," and notice how that feels in your body.

"I'm figuring it out," creates space for options, hope, possibilities, doing the damn thing, and taking back the power you gave away to someone or a situation.

Practice this small tweak and reap big rewards!

CHAPTER 43

How to Meditate – Or Not!

When meditation came on the scene in popular culture, some asshole made it sound like we should be able to shut our brains off when we do it. And we believed them because they're the "expert." We believed that if you're not able to shut your brain off while meditating, then you're doing it wrong or there's something wrong with you.

Talk about setting yourself up for "failure!" Our brains are designed and wired to function 24/7 or we will die. Hard stop. It's not that some "successful" meditators can shut their brains off while the rest of us are big dummies who never get to have inner peace or nirvana because *our* brains go non-stop. Even the most seasoned and practiced meditators have human brains just like me and you; they run, hum, and operate constantly.

The difference is that some people, meditators or not, have practiced and learned how to turn the volume down on their brain's messages. They don't believe everything they think, and they don't make their brain's "non-stopness" a problem. Because they do those things a little more than others, they don't get sucked into their brain's drama and shenanigans on endless loops.

I love sharing this tidbit because everyone who hears it, feels less alone and broken. They thought there was something wrong with them that they couldn't get more than three seconds of quiet time between their ears. Their faces and jaws relax too as they realize their experience is the norm and that their goal was misguided from the start.

You can turn the volume down on your thoughts, messages, and voices that run through your brain like a school closing message at the bottom of your TV. But shut it off? Nope. It's not necessary and there's no need to try. For me, just realizing that "shutting my brain off" isn't possible, was such a relief and helped to quiet things down.

Let yourself off the hook. Want to give meditation another try? Go for it and keep it super simple.

- You can use an app like Calm for guided meditations of all lengths.
- You don't need a cushion, Zen room, incense, special music, or a gong. A comfortable chair and your phone is enough.
- Literally start with setting a timer on your phone for one minute. Put your hands wherever they're comfortable, and close your eyes.
- Take a deep but comfortable breath in through your nose if possible, and exhale either through your nose or through pursed lips; it looks like you're going to kiss someone.
- When–not if–thoughts come, just let them go like you're noticing a cloud floating by. This one piece allows you to become the watcher of your thoughts, and helps you see that you are not your thoughts. Notice the thought and let it go. Notice and let go, over and over until the timer goes off.
- Doing this at the beginning of your day will help to calm your nervous system, lower your blood pressure, help you see that you are not your thoughts, and bring you out of your primitive brain, fight/flight/freeze, and into your prefrontal cortex.

Not your thing? That's cool. There are loads of other things that accomplish the same goal without sitting down and closing your eyes:

- You could go for a walk.
- Sip coffee and listen to a favorite playlist.
- Journal (nothing fancy or specific, jotting down your thoughts is awesome).
- Watch hysterical reels until you almost pee your pants.
- Call your BFF.
- Play with your furry kids.

There are countless activities you can do to give your brain a rest, get back into your body, and notice and let go of your thoughts. The only thing that matters is that you enjoy it. Being a little more present in the moment and not getting totally sucked into believing your thoughts is all you're going for. Keep it simple and do what feels good to you.

Stop searching for your brain's off switch. It doesn't have one, and that's not a problem.

CHAPTER 44

Expand Your Focus

When we feel threatened or stressed, our focus narrows. It's a primal response and one many of us do without realizing we're doing it or why. It helps us pay very close attention to what may be threatening us and our survival. But being hyper-focused is an overwhelming way to live. It keeps stress hormones pumping through our systems and our brains and bodies on high alert.

We develop hyper focus as a survival technique. Our brains sense threats to our safety so it activates our fight/flight/freeze response. For some of us this response is often on 24/7 and can stay on indefinitely until we begin to work with our nervous systems, via somatic practices, to create a sense of safety.

Hyper focus can look like:

- Being aware of the slightest change in someone's temperament or emotional state.
- Very sensitive hearing or what I call being able to hear a mouse fart.
- Big startle responses.
- Checking in with "your person" multiple times to make sure they're ok because if "they're ok, you're ok."
- Obsessing over what you said at a party, during a meeting, or in an email.
- Focusing on someone else instead of living your big beautiful life.
- Always being "on" and having a hard time relaxing.

None of these are bad or wrong. They're maladaptive survival techniques that our brains come up with in order to protect us from scary shit in our lives. I did every single one of them for a very long time, until I did the work in this book, so that I do them less and less. You can do that too!

We can apply this pattern in reverse to help calm our alarm and help regulate our emotions and nervous systems. When our focus widens, it signals a sense of safety and security to our bodies and brains.

- Focus on a point in front of you. You can do this sitting, standing, or walking.
- Then allow your focus to widen and go out a foot or so.
- And then expand your focus another foot.
- And another foot.
- And then go all the way to the edges of your peripheral vision.
- You can go back to your focal point and repeat the steps if you'd like. Your call.

Do this throughout your day to calm and soothe your nervous system so it can have evidence that it's safe to relax. Practicing this technique will wire it into your brain and it'll become another helpful tool in your toolbox. Do it when you're in the bathroom. I like linking activities together because it makes them easier to remember and you're in the bathroom a handful of times a day anyway.

CHAPTER 45

Put Yourself Back in The Driver's Seat

We're dependent on someone else for our survival from the moment we're conceived. Our umbilical cord gives us what we need to develop and grow, and our mother's body gives us protection. When we're born we need others to meet our basic needs of food, shelter, clothing, safety, and love.

Unfortunately most of us aren't taught how to take over the responsibility of taking care of ourselves in healthy ways, at age-appropriate times. We're taught to keep looking outside ourselves for love, attention, reassurance, and our general feeling of ok-ness. We don't learn that it can, and needs to, come from ourselves first. Then all the other good stuff from others are sprinkles on the cupcake.

When we believe that all the good stuff comes from outside ourselves:

- We give our power, money, and energy to boyfriends, girlfriends, parents, lotions, pills, and diet plans we think will make us feel better, or at least not as bad, but will never get the job done. This is a losing battle.
- We don't learn how to show up for ourselves when we're feeling anxious or any other "big scary" emotion. We don't know that we can sit with and process our feelings in 90 seconds, so we look outside for solutions to something going on inside.
- We need other people to tell us we're important, special, smart, and loved because we don't believe we are.

- We keep trying to fill a hole with people and stuff that can never do the job.

Looking outside ourselves, giving our power away, and not being in the driver's seat are learned habits for our survival. We all did it. Our habits helped ensure we'd be accepted by our pack and allowed to stay. It's been passed down from one generation to the next, and we aren't going to waste time on useless things like blame, shame, and judgment. Your habits can *always* be changed with small tweaks and practice. That's all it takes.

What it can look like to kick yourself out of the driver's seat:

- Saying "yes" when you want to say "no." We could list a zillion examples, amiright?!
- Keeping your mouth shut instead of calling someone out for their rude comment.
- Saying you don't care what your family has for dinner when you're craving tacos like crazy.
- You want to go to the beach for your family's vacation but cave when someone else says they want to go skiing.
- You have a great solution for a problem at work but don't offer it up because you're scared everyone will think it's dumb.
- Wanting to set a boundary with a family member but don't because you haven't done it before, and you're terrified of what will happen.
- Staying small and quiet when there's really a tiger inside that is ready to explode.

It can be easy to start yelling about how we got here and rage against people and systems. Have those big feelings and then like one of my fave refrigerator magnets says, "Put on your big girl panties and deal with it!"

It's not our fault that we got here, we did it to survive, *and* it is our responsibility to change it. No one is going to rescue us and we don't need them to. We are 100% capable of doing it. We just forgot. We gave our power away so slowly we didn't realize it happened.

Why should you sit your own ass back in the seat?

It's *your* seat, *your* throne, and only *you* belong there!

The following things are helping me get back in my driver's seat:

- I've come to love the hell outta striving for B- work instead of A+! I'm listening to myself when it feels like the thing is "good enough," and I send it off.
- I used to believe I needed to "get rid" of anxiety to have a good life, and boy howdy did I spend oodles of time and money on that futile and unnecessary pursuit. Uff-da! Now I believe it's a normal emotion and signal that I need to pay attention to something.
- Listen less to ads that tell me I'm not peachy just as I am. Ads that tell me, "If I just buy their thing-y, everything will be rainbows and butterflies, I'll finally feel like I have my shit together, everyone will love me, my dogs will be perfectly behaved, I'll never argue with my wife, I'll reach my goal weight, and never feel bad again." We're smart enough to know we don't believe those lies, but a part of us *really does* or we wouldn't put trillions of dollars in the pockets of big companies every year!
- I spend a little time most days watching Facebook reels that make me laugh, often snort, and occasionally pee a little. This reminds me that fun is important and life

doesn't have to be as serious as my brain tells me it is.

- When I remember I'm a pack animal who doesn't want to be left behind, I can remind myself that I don't need to compare and keep up with people in my social media feeds. This allows me to be my weird and unique self instead of making myself look and act a certain way.

I want you to get curious. Put your detective or scientist hat on and collect some data. Who are the people currently in your driver's seat? It's often a number of people and they rotate depending on the situation. It could be your mom, boss, sister, someone from middle school, Karen from the PTA board, your dad, spouse, your kids, or co-worker, or a generic list of "shoulds."

You get to decide every day, often many times a day, if they get to stay there or if you're going to evict them and sit your own ass back down. The choice is always yours, you just forgot.

When I see you in your driver's seat, I'll honk atcha from mine! And I hope you like 80's music because that'll be blasting out my car windows! We got this!

CHAPTER 46

We Train People How to Treat Us

We train people how to treat us. Period. Hard stop.

We don't want to believe this because then we'd have to take responsibility and maybe make changes, but it's true.

When I kept taking my first boyfriend back after he cheated on me, not once, but twice and gave me an STD, I was training him that that behavior was acceptable. I told him it wasn't, and tried to put a boundary in place, but I didn't adhere to it at all. That showed him it was ok. I would say one thing but do another.

When someone speaks to me or treats me in an unkind way, and I don't say anything, or say something that's passive aggressive, I'm training them that it's ok to do so.

I used to keep my words and real feelings down with food, sugar, or alcohol. They were like a stopper. I didn't say what was really on my mind and heart because I was afraid that if I did, the important people in my life would get mad and leave physically or emotionally. And my alarm/primitive brain saw that as certain death.

I also want to point out the glaring fact that those of us socialized as women were shushed, beaten, killed, shamed, and institutionalized for speaking up and out. As bananas as it may sound, our nervous systems remember this! It gets wired into us and passed down from one generation to the next, which affects our thoughts, feelings, and actions to this day!

So when someone makes a snide comment at work, it's your responsibility to speak up for yourself in the moment or after, if that's what you feel called to do. You can do this with a kindness that you weren't given. You could say something like, "It's not ok for you to speak to me like that, and if it continues, I'm ending the conversation or talking to your boss about it." You don't have to return their rude comment with one of your own.

Most of us are not used to direct communication. It can come across as rude, mean, unkind, or too straightforward. But I think indirect communication causes so many *more* problems and suffering internally and in our relationships.

The more I communicate directly the better I feel about myself.

- My belief grows that what I want/need to say is important.
- My self-worth increases because I'm raising my standards for how I treat myself and how I will allow others to treat me.
- My self-confidence grows as I practice new boundaries.
- My relationships improve because things aren't going unsaid, which always leads to resentment and problems.
- My frustration levels are lower because I'm asking for help, what I want and need, instead of suffering in silence hoping someone will rescue me.
- I'm treating myself and others like the grown-ass adults we are instead of over-functioning and treating them like helpless children.

This takes practice, peeps! Practice showing up for yourself. Practice putting a new boundary in place and following through with what you said you're going to do.

This isn't comfortable because it's new and brains don't like new things. It's also uncomfortable because it goes against *many* years of socialization; the only way to change it is to take little kitten steps in the direction you want to go. Your brain will start to see that you won't die by speaking a little more directly.

It's just like a muscle you're trying to strengthen by lifting weights. You don't go to the gym and try to bench press 200 pounds if you've never done it before. Don't start this practice by trying to set three big boundaries with your MIL.

Since most of us interact with humans on the regular, start noticing where you feel frustrated, annoyed, or overwhelmed. Where would you like to be more direct? There's always a kind-ish way to say something. It's not a case where you either say nothing or completely lose your shit. There's lots of middle ground.

A great place to start is when you're being asked what you'd like for dinner. If pasta sounds good, say that. If you're asked what you'd like to watch on TV, and you want to know what's going on with the new season of *Survivor*, say that. Start small and build that muscle. It might sound unrelated, but this also builds your "noticing what you want/need" and your "speaking up" muscles.

We train people how to treat us. And if you don't like how you've trained someone, it's time to tweak it and practice more direct communication.

CHAPTER 47

Outsourcing Emotional Needs

Sometimes coaching involves tough love because our brains will believe their bullshit forever if we keep the story going and don't question it.

On a coaching call one of my clients said her husband doesn't value her. She explained how his actions were making her feel pissed and unappreciated.

I asked her:

- Do *you* value *you*? Do you see how and where you're expecting yourself to do all the things all the time and have a psychotic smile on your face like nothing is wrong?
- Are *you* showing up for yourself? Or are *you* expecting your partner to read your mind or body language to see how stressed you are and come to your rescue?
- What are you wanting *him* to do for you that you're not doing for yourself? Like saying you want a break from your kids before someone snaps your last nerve.

Those might have stung a little *and* they're really important to ask yourself or you'll stay pissed and stuck.

When she set aside the judgment about her husband's actions, and got curious about her thought and feeling loop, she saw how she was outsourcing her value and not speaking up for herself. It has to start with you. If you're wanting something from someone else, it might be in part because you're not giving it to yourself.

It's not someone else's responsibility to affirm, praise, encourage, support, and take care of all of your emotional needs. That's being an emotional child.

That's not to say we don't want, need, and appreciate those things. We're pack animals and hearing praise or feeling supported feels amazing because that releases happy chemicals like oxytocin into our bloodstream. The problem comes when we only look outside ourselves for praise and support and rarely, if ever, do them for ourselves. That puts a lot of pressure on the other person and the relationship can get out of balance and unhealthy. And what happens if the relationship ends or changes somehow? Then you're up shit creek without a paddle because you put all your eggs in one basket and you'll do the same thing with the next person.

You need to see your own value first, that is your responsibility. You need to practice being your own cheerleader, friend, and advocate first. Then when you do get that good stuff from others, it's like sprinkles on your cupcake. But you have to do the work to give yourself the cupcake in the first place.

Outsourcing your emotional needs gives away your power. This causes loads of suffering because you start doing mental gymnastics and unconscious manipulation to try to get others to give you what you want. You'll wind up exhausted and feeling like a powerless victim. Been there, done that. Zero stars, do not recommend.

Because awareness is queen, and 95% of our thoughts are unconscious, I gave my client the homework to notice when she was outsourcing a feeling to her husband or wanting him to fix something without her saying that.

Her next step was to ask how she could give that to herself. What are a few things she thinks are pretty kick ass about her? What are some examples of how she's killin' it? What is she handling like a boss? She needed to start celebrating herself and be her own cheerleader. She needs to do both. Celebrate herself *and* speak up.

Whatever it is that you want so badly from others, you have to practice giving it to yourself first, or what you get from the outside will never be enough, or stick. It'll be like giving a super dry plant a bunch of water, it'll run right through the parched dirt.

Then, decide if it's time to talk about workloads, division of labor, or whatever is truly on your heart and mind. This is usually a multi-layered situation and that's ok because life isn't black-and-white. It's all the beautiful colors in the middle.

CHAPTER 48

Could Versus Should

I love catching up with other life coaches. It's fun to be able to geek out about brain stuff and coachy stuff with people who love it as much as I do. During one such catch-up session, my friend Gabriel Garofalo said, "the words 'should' comes from shame, and the word 'could' comes from creation."

I immediately said, "Tell me more about that!" She went on to explain that when we're "shoulding" ourselves, that's coming from shaming energy. It's punitive, shrinking, and does not get us motivated or going in the direction we want. But when we "could" ourselves, that's coming from an energy of creation, opportunity, options, and expansion.

Say "could" and "should" to yourself; see how you feel, and how your body responds. The words have very different weight and energy. To me, "should" feels heavy, dark, restrictive, and sticky like when you get Christmas tree sap on your fingers and have to use Goo Gone to get it off. "Should" can also be very manipulative. It's a sneaky, fly-under-the-radar way for others to get you to doubt yourself and do what they think is best. Which is probably not what's best for you. "Could," on the other hand, feels light, airy, expansive, curious, and full of options. It feels playful, freeing, and creative.

We have a choice which word we use when we talk to ourselves and others. If you're like the rest of us, "should" is a pretty common part of your vocabulary. Start noticing when you say it. Don't beat yourself up, just notice because you're collecting data.

Then try switching the words. It'll take practice and that's ok. You've simply created the default pattern of saying, "should," and you can easily practice replacing it with, "could."

How do these thoughts feel in your body?

- I should do more cardio.
- I should want to play with my kids more.
- I should eat more veggies.
- I should call my mom more.
- I should say yes to being on the committee at school.
- I should walk my dogs more.
- I should go to my in-laws for holidays.
- I should be less judgy.
- I should go into work on my day off because they're short-staffed.
- I should wear something other than leggings.
- I should meditate, journal, do yoga.

Versus, how do the following thoughts feel in your body?

- I could do more cardio, but I prefer lifting some weights and leisure walks.
- I could play with my kids more, and it's ok that it's not my fave activity. It's important that they learn independence, and we spend lots of quality time together in other ways.
- I could add a simple salad a few times a week because that's doable and I like them.
- I could call my mom more, but she always nitpicks my weight and what I wear, so I'm going to limit those conversations for my mental health.
- I could wait and agree to be on a committee that interests me instead of one that would bore me to tears.

- I could walk my dogs once a week to start. Some is better than none.
- I could go to my in-laws for the holidays but stay at a hotel so we can have space and time to ourselves.
- I could get curious and ask myself where the judging is coming from, and remind myself that brains are wired to look for the negative, i.e. judge, and I can tweak that habit.
- I could remind myself that the situation at work is not my responsibility and I'm already feeling burnt out so I'm going to rest at home.
- I could wear something other than leggings but they're amazing and versatile so I'm going to keep wearing them.
- I could meditate, journal, and do yoga *if* I feel called to do them and it's 100% ok if I don't.

How do the "could" versions of the thoughts feel in your body? Lighter, less shame-y, and like options instead of punishments?

There's another word swap I want you to ponder and practice.

When I think about things I *have* to do, I take on this whiny, toddler-like pouty attitude, and all I can think is, "I don't wanna…" I drag my feet, find half a dozen other things to do instead of the thing that needs to get done, and all the while feeling weighed down by responsibility and adulting. Blech.

On the flip side, when I think about things I *choose* to do, I may still not want to do them, but I'm not pouting or procrastinating. There's a lighter, can-do feeling that isn't making something worse because of the other shit I'm telling myself and piling on top. There's also an element of empowerment in "choose to" that is absent in "have to." When we make a conscious choice about something, it strengthens our autonomy and feeling like we have control in our lives because we do, even when we don't see it.

Run these examples through your body and see how they feel:

- I have to pick up the dog's poop.
- I have to pay my taxes.
- I have to do the laundry.
- I have to get gas.
- I have to take the car in for maintenance.
- I have to change the kid's sheets because they threw up/ had an accident.

How did each of those feel? Maybe heavy, daunting, or overwhelming.

Now, run these thoughts through your body and see how they feel:

- I choose to pick up the dog's poop so the yard isn't covered and they don't eat it (sheesh I hate when ours do that!).
- I choose to pay my taxes because I don't want to pay penalties or wind up in the clink.
- I choose to do the laundry so everyone has clean clothes. This can also be delegated or tweaked to be less of a burden.
- I choose to get gas because I don't want to run out and have to call someone or AAA.
- I choose to take the car in for its maintenance so it doesn't break down and cost more in the long run.
- I choose to change the kid's sheets because dirty sheets suck.

How did each of those feel? I know they didn't suddenly make you jump for joy at doing them, and that's not what we're going for. But substituting "choose" for "have," probably made them suck less, which is what we're going for. Kitten steps right?

I want you to see the bigger picture, that you're not a victim in your life. You may have been at the mercy of others when you were a child, but now you're a grown-ass adult who gets to decide how to show up to your life.

I'm really excited for you to try these word swaps. Take it slow and see how it goes. I bet you're going to feel less self-judgment and like you have more options in your life.

You got this!

CHAPTER 49

Move Your Body

I had a request for some "legit, get your ass off the couch, exercise hacks." Roger that, and here they come, along with some important background details.

Every action you take, or don't take, is because of our thought/feeling loop; it drives us. You have a thought, that thought creates a feeling, and that feeling leads to an action, and sometimes that action is inaction. Or, you're feeling something, which leads you to think something and that thought leads to an action, and sometimes that action is inaction.

What are your thoughts and feelings about exercise? Are they along the lines of, "I hate doing this, it's torture, I don't have time, I'm not seeing results fast enough?" Or frustration, defeatist, and annoyed. Those thoughts and feelings will not help get you off the couch. Start to notice what you're thinking and feeling to decide if they're serving you.

The way through this issue is by combining the brilliance of the body and brain. Doing one without the other won't get you where you want to be. Practice one or more of the somatic exercises to calm and soothe your alarm and nervous system, and release the energy of the thought and feeling. When the charged energy has decreased and you're in your prefrontal cortex, you can decide what you'd rather think that's a little less shitty and what doable kitten step you want to take next.

Examples of thoughts about exercise that are a little less shitty are:

- This won't last forever.
- I'll be happy that I did it.
- I'll feel better about myself after.
- It's a step in the direction I want to go.

It's also really important to have a compelling "why." *Why* is it important to you to get your ass off the couch? Because it's so much easier to stay where you are or come up with seven other things you could do instead of exercise. Suddenly cleaning out your kitchen's junk drawer seems really important and kind of fun, amiright?

Sit down and ask yourself *why* you want to get off the couch. You'll hear an answer if you listen. Then ask why, to that answer. Keep going for at least five rounds of "why." It usually takes that many to get to the real, meaty, deep down reason. The reason that will be compelling enough to tear you away from another episode of the show you're binging. Your "why" needs to be more than, "I want to fit in my jeans," because it won't be hard to say, "Oh I'll just get a bigger size." Go deeper to find your honest "why."

The primitive part of our brains, the limbic system, keeps us alive by decreasing physical and emotional pain, increasing pleasure, and doing everything as efficiently as possible.

These are good reasons it's hard to get your ass off the couch. Your brain knows that if you stay home, don't go outside where there's danger, you'll stay alive. We have a legit, lifesaving, 650 million-year-old system at play, that we have to be aware of in order to override. Otherwise you're going to think you're lazy, beat yourself up, and want to stay on the couch.

Now you have your "why," you know what's going on in your brain, and you have a thought to practice when the old one wants to run the show. Your new thought will take practice because the old, crappy, and unhelpful thoughts are your default. Keep practicing even when you think it's not working. When you do the somatic practices and keep thinking your new thought, it'll get stronger and quickly become your new normal thought and the old one will get weaker.

Next it's time to ask yourself how you can make moving your body more fun. Those might include:

- New, comfy shoes if your others have seen better days, and have them ready to go, not hiding in your closet.
- Comfortable clothes that are weather appropriate if you're outside and have them ready to put on.
- Create a fun playlist that really fires you up. Maybe podcasts are your jam. Music and podcasts help me keep moving.
- What do you enjoy doing? Maybe you're making yourself do something you don't like. The important thing is to move your body more. Period. You don't have to do spin classes if they're not your thing. Find something you enjoy and do it more. Sometimes I have a solo dance party at home while my dogs look at me like I've lost my damn mind.
- Celebrate every time you do it! Start training your brain to focus on what you're doing and accomplishing. Celebrate the hell out of that! When you do, your brain and body will want to do it more. What we celebrate, we integrate!

Motivation builds on itself. It doesn't fall from the sky, we don't suddenly wake up with it, and it does not come in a box from Amazon. Try some of these ideas to see what works for you.

The hardest step is the first one. It gets easier from there, and you can do this!

CHAPTER 50

Ask Yourself Helpful Questions

Our brains are amazing, phenomenal, spectacular problem-solving machines! Brains put the most advanced computer to shame with their capacity. Our brains love to solve problems so much they'll actually *create* a problem so it has something to do. This is one reason people worry so much. That and worrying *feels* helpful because we believe we're working on a solution. But we're not, we're just ruminating.

One thing our brains do to try to give us something to work on is to ask unhelpful questions.

Examples of unhelpful questions are:

- What's wrong with me?
- Why can't I figure this out?
- Why do I keep doing this over and over?
- Why does he/she/they keep doing that?
- When am I going to get my shit together?
- Why is this happening to me?

How do these questions feel in your body when you read them? Heavy, dark, shame-inducing, like you want to crawl under a rock? Do they look familiar? I've asked myself those questions countless times and not once did they lead to self-awareness or a better outcome.

This type of question is not helpful. They're vague enough and blaming that they keep you spinning in circles scrounging for clarity. They don't get you going in the direction you want to go. Instead they pile on a metric ton of shame, judgment, and keep you stuck in quicksand feeling like a pathetic loser. At least that was my experience.

A better alternative is to put your big, beautiful brain to work in a helpful way. A way that will focus on what you can change and get you going in the direction you want to go.

Examples of helpful questions:

- What is in my control?
- What worked, didn't work, and what do I want to do differently next time?
- When have I figured out something like this in the past and how can I apply it now?
- How can I make this simpler, easier, or more fun?

How do these questions feel in your body when you read them? Empowering, lighter, expansive?

Let me give you an example. One sweet client asked, "Why can't I get motivated to tidy up my house or get back to the gym after I was sick?" Ninety-nine percent of the answer has to do with the question she asked.

She's *solving for the wrong "problem."* Her brain is looking for the reasons she *"can't"* get motivated. And because brains love to solve problems, it's going to pile up a whole bunch of reasons to help you solve the problem. And those reasons are going to feel like crap.

- Confirmation bias causes us to look for evidence to prove we're right to save ourselves emotional and physical energy. This is the primitive brain wanting to be efficient to ensure our survival in case we need it to fend off a tiger. It really believes this, pinky promise.

- Then we feel bad because of all the BS answers our brains came up with.
- If we're not aware of our brain's shenanigans, we'll keep making choices that perpetuate the same thought/feeling loop to keep the efficiency going.
- If you're asking yourself a question and as a result you're thinking shameful and judgemental thought, and you feel like crap, it's unhelpful.
- Instead, ditch the emotion and ask yourself one of the questions from the above "helpful questions" list.

I *love* knowing how we tick and why, because that knowledge is power! We can do something with it. We can take our power and control back and change our lives!

My client and I went on to chat more about what was going on in her thought/feeling loop, and what she can do differently to get back to the gym and tidy up her house. Hear me out, it's not about swapping pie-in-the-sky thoughts for the crappy ones. It's about somatic practices to process the feelings in your body and thinking thoughts that are a little less shitty, so you get better results. No shootin'-for-the-moon thoughts because your brain won't believe them and you'll be right back on the couch with a messy house. When we learn what's going on in our precious noggins and tend to the emotions in our body we're going to heal what's going on instead of just applying a temporary band-aid.

Our brains are wired and designed to change, neuroplasticity. With practice you can change patterns that are new-ish or decades old!

CHAPTER 51

Let Go of Judgment

How are you using the thing?

For example, a couple coaching clients are keeping track of what they're eating and how they feel physically and emotionally after eating. There are two main ways they can use the information they gather:

- As a way to punish and beat themselves up, or evidence that they're not doing enough and doing it all wrong.
- Or as data, information, clues, and things to look at deeper.

The latter will get you so much further and just takes practice.

In this example, my clients are just writing down items of food. A list that could look like: cereal, milk and a banana. A cheeseburger, fries, and a chocolate malt. Salmon and basmati rice. A handful of peanut M&M's, chips, and queso dip.

In all reality, the list is completely and 100% neutral.

But it's all the shame, guilt, and blame you pile on top of the list of neutral food items that keep you stuck and from taking different actions if that's what you want.

I tell myself and my clients that we're going to be detectives and scientists. I loved the 1980's cartoon character and show, *Inspector Gadget*, and his always-saving-the-day, niece Penny and her dog Brain. He's who I think of when I go detective-y with myself. I think of Sully when I go science-y because she's a retired science teacher and I imagine her leading a lab in class.

We're just collecting data, numbers, and information. Looking at something this way will turn down the volume on judgment, shame, and blame! And when we turn the volume down on judgment, shame, and blame, we can make decisions that serve us better and get us going in the direction we want.

We're going to kindly refocus our brains when they want to default to judgment, shame, and blame. Our brains are used to operating this way because it's a familiar habit and now you're tweaking it and doing it differently.

Remember, brains don't want you to use energy to think differently, because you may need that energy to fend off a tiger or bear. That's what the primitive part of your brain legit thinks.

When you look at things as data instead of ammunition against yourself, it's a *wealth* of information because you're not making it mean something bad about you. Your value, worthiness, and lovability do not hinge on information you gather. We're used to thinking the information *absolutely* means something about us. I invite you to be open to the possibility that that is just an error in how we've all been operating and thinking.

We can choose how we look at something; it's our responsibility to change our perspective if it isn't serving us or giving us the results we want. There isn't only one way of looking at something; the choice is always ours. We can look at the data, decide what we're going to do with it, and slowly make changes.

Keep the data! Ditch the drama, judgment, blaming, shaming, and staying stuck.

CHAPTER 52

Finding Confidence

Are you waiting to do the thing until you feel more confident?

Most of us have confidence ass-backwards.

We believe we need to wait to do the thing until we feel more confident.

- I'll ask for a promotion when I feel more confident.
- I'll start a business, podcast, or side job, when I feel more confident.
- I'll have the hard convo when I feel more confident.
- I'll go back to the gym when I feel more confident.

Waiting for the confidence to magically fall from the sky only delays you from getting what you want. It's like we're waiting for Amazon, the Universe, God, a parent, or someone, to *give* us confidence because we're socialized to look outside ourselves for basically everything.

Instead, realize that confidence is like a muscle that we strengthen with practice and use.

You don't *get* confidence first and then go do the thing *next*.

You do the thing, your confidence muscle grows, and then it's easier to do the next thing.

I started a podcast with very little confidence. I didn't have fancy equipment, an editor, an intro or outro. I had an inexpensive mic, a desire to share what I know in a new medium, and I had "permission" from a mentor to do it imperfectly.

Permission to just start with what I had that would get the job done. I didn't wait until I felt confident because I knew I needed to do the thing and the confidence would grow naturally.

I quit looking for all my confidence, reassurance, and "atta-girls" outside myself. Instead, I got to work doing the thing and slowly watched my confidence grow, and gave myself "attagirls" along the way.

Don't wait to do the thing until you're 100% confident. If you wait you'll never do it because 100% confidence is a perfectionistic lie that'll keep you exactly where you are.

Take some kitten steps in the direction you want to go, and watch how your confidence muscles grow. Just like Popeye's arms when he'd have some spinach!

You got this!

CHAPTER 53

Would You Say That to a Toddler?

We get *so* frustrated and annoyed with ourselves when it takes us a hot minute to change a behavior. We expect that because we "know" something and we've made the decision to do the thing that should just already be a done deal, damn it. And to hell with any grace, compassion, or understanding that we're learning a new habit or thought. Nope, none of that for you.

Sound familiar?

Our society is used to, and very comfortable with, using punishment to try to change behavior. Look at our prison system. That isn't working so well either. Fear of punishment or punishment itself isn't an effective way to change behavior. If it was, we'd be changing things left and right, and they'd stick. Beating ourselves up only perpetuates what we don't want because it creates shame that keeps us in our unhelpful cycles. But we just keep doubling down on trash-talking ourselves thinking *this* time it'll work. It won't.

When a toddler is learning to walk, they're not expected to try once and then never fall on their butt or face plant. No, we give them all the sweetness, kiss their boo-boos, cheer them on, and hug them as they struggle to learn and practice a *new-to-them* thing. We wouldn't dream of yelling at them, telling them to hurry up and figure it out, or say, "You've tried once, why can't you walk yet?!"

Keep this analogy front and center when you're working on doing something new or in a different way. I don't care what it is.

- Incorporating more movement into your routine? Take it slow and steady and celebrate what you get done.

- Creating boundaries with your in-laws? Listen to what your gut is telling you, start small, and high-five yourself when you follow through instead of caving.
- Wanting to be one percent more compassionate with yourself? Stop when you realize you're trash talking yourself and say one nice thing to your sweet being.
- Spent the whole night awake while your mind was spinning? Write the following trick on a post-it note and put it on your nightstand. Slowly count backward from 100. I do it every night to help me fall asleep. Sometimes I get down to one and start over, no big deal. Sometimes I don't remember getting to 80.

No matter what the new habit, thought, or tweak is, treat yourself like you would a toddler learning to walk. Be a little more sweet and compassionate with yourself.

I *know* you'll get there!

CHAPTER 54

Have More Fun!

One of the coolest things I've learned is that playing and having fun is calming and soothing to our internal alarms/nervous systems. Having fun and playing are signs to our bodies and brains that we're safe and therefore help us to quiet our alarms and soothe ourselves. Yay, who wants to play UNO?!

On the flip side, when we're on high alert or hyper vigilant, which I know a lot about, that's a signal to our systems that we aren't safe and need to maintain those states in order to ensure our safety, in case a tiger jumps out. Play can be a beautiful cycle. When we play and have fun, it tells us that we're safe, which perpetuates more fun and safety. I'd much rather be in the fun cycle instead of the high alert cycle.

There were a few times in my childhood where I was yelled at pretty intensely for what happened when I was having fun, so fun started to equal danger. I erred on the side of "let's not make a mess, don't be too much, be quiet, let's wait to see their reaction before I do anything." Those warnings were my body's alarm attempting to keep me safe and they did. But they also held me back from being a kid. I would often watch the other kids in my neighborhood with *awe* at how they'd just play, imagine, and be themselves.

So on my current path of befriending my brain and body, I'm intentionally bringing in more fun. I'll ask Sully to play UNO or Sorry, watch my favorite movie, *Zootopia*, or scroll videos on social media and share the ones that make me laugh-cry. I've "tasked" myself with having more fun, and it feels really good.

Each time I play and have fun, I'm rewiring my brain. I'm showing it that I'm safe in this moment, that I can have fun and nothing bad will happen, and I'm practicing being present with my alarm no matter what. It felt a little scary and uncomfortable in the beginning because of my previous wiring; now I've gotten a lot more comfortable with it and it feels good, cozy, and like a sweet treat that I'm giving myself.

I bet you could use more fun and play in your life. What is one small way you can start? Kitten steps, Sunshine, kitten steps.

CHAPTER 55

Drop into Your Body

The purpose of somatic (body) practices is to calm your alarm/ nervous system, create a greater sense of comfort and safety in your body, rewire your brain's default habit pathways, and therefore be able to call up that tool and comfort when you want/ need it. You're probably up in your head right now, so I invite you to drop down into your body by practicing a technique one of my coaches, Victoria Albina, calls: "This is my arm."

With one hand, gently squeeze your other hand, and at the same time say, "This is my hand." Move up your arm, squeezing and saying, "This is my wrist, this is my forearm, this is my elbow, etc." Saying the body part while squeezing it, brings you out of your squirrely brain and back into your body. This gives your brain the chance to realize you're not in danger, and will be more open to your invitation to calm down.

You can move on to using both hands and slowly do the same thing over your torso, head, and legs. Gently squeezing and saying the body part to yourself or out loud. You can do this anywhere which is one thing I love about many somatic practices. You can be in a meeting, the car, a bathroom stall, and no one will know what you're doing. Kids can do them while at school to help themselves. They're simple, free, and effective.

When we're in our bodies, it sends a gentle reminder to our alarm/primitive brain that we can calm down because it has learned over 650 million years of evolution that being in our bodies as opposed to our brain, means we're safer. We can take a deep breath, our minds can get quieter, and we chill.

Practicing this technique throughout the day is a great way to grow your sense of calm and safety.

CHAPTER 56

Unleash Your Feminine Energy

I started my coaching practice to help people. I wanted to share the life-changing information I had learned and used to tweak things I never thought I could tweak. Like waking up with anxiety every morning, constantly throwing myself under the bus to try to make everyone happy so then I could be happy, and start to make choices that lit me up.

I had shit to do, stuff to say, and lives to help change!

I had already been running and loving my massage therapy practice for 26 years but I wanted to get the word out about my new adventure in the best, fastest, and smartest ways possible. I wanted to learn and heard about a handful of coaches who were killing in the field. One of them in particular was a business coach so she seemed like the logical person. She had what I wanted; a successful coaching practice that was supporting women to create lives they loved and not ones they constantly wanted to escape.

I followed her on social media, read her emails, and bought her course. She had protocols to follow, scripts to use, videos to watch, and PDFs to fill out. I thought, "Yes, I have the instructions and manual for how to do this, I'm set, let's fucking go!"

Except it didn't feel good. I had plugged in my details and was chugging away but wasn't getting the results I wanted. Some of her suggestions were way out of my comfort zone and not my personality at all. I'm all about stretching my comfort zone, but some ideas felt like I was being body checked by a professional hockey player out of my comfort zone. I kept my nose to the ground, analyzed my results, I was disciplined, and followed her map. All the while praying it would get easier, more fun, more successful, and feel better. It didn't.

The more I followed the coach's suggestions the more I felt like I was wearing a too-tight wool sweater, and I'm very allergic to wool. I felt like *I* was doing something wrong, like *I* was the problem, and I just needed to try her way a *little* harder and then things would click.

I was exhausted, frustrated, and not in the headspace I wanted to be in when I realized my bigger problem. I was hard-core in my masculine energy and had completely shoved aside my strong feminine energy. I wasn't having much fun, being playful or creative, and I sure as shit wasn't following my intuition. I was pushing and forcing instead of allowing and being open to cool things coming my way.

Ideally we're a mixture of masculine and feminine, and can call upon one or the other when we need more of either energy depending on the situation. Both are important, beautiful, strong, and get 'er done energy but they go about it in different ways. Feminine energy has been looked upon as weak, submissive, emotional, ineffective, and given the stink face. It's anything but!

Let's look at both. Masculine energy encourages us to be:

- Protective
- Single-focused
- Purpose-driven
- Analytical
- Practical
- Logical
- Competitive
- Structured
- Disciplined
- Focused outside ourselves

Whereas feminine energy encourages us to be:

- Compassionate
- Magnetic
- Open
- Creative
- Intuitive
- Sensitive
- Nurturing
- Trusting
- Empathetic
- Receptive

As I was starting out and wanting to do things the "right way," I was solidly operating from my masculine side. I was operating from a forceful, pushing energy. It felt like a very inflexible way to start and grow a practice that I was so excited to bring to the world. And I felt very out of balance. Like when you're really dehydrated and your electrolytes are off. I felt wobbly and off inside.

There was little to no creativity, intuition, magnetism, openness, or trust to what I was doing. I was trying to check off boxes to do things the "right" way, and impatiently waiting for clients to hire me.

There was another fairy godmother of a coach, Simone Seol, on my radar. Her message was different from the first coach. I interpreted Simone's message as *listen to what feels fun and good to your body, have fun and play around with your content, trust yourself and your potential clients, and fuck all the other messages out there including mine if it goes against your intuition.*

This was the affirming permission slip I needed to do things my way! If it didn't feel good, right, aligned, and in integrity with my core, I didn't do it. I broke the rules! I burned the rule book and created my own and it was so fucking liberating and freeing! I felt like a huge weight was lifted off my shoulders and no one was looking over my shoulder anymore ready to crack a whip because I wasn't following the manual.

It's not breaking news that we've been eyeballs-deep in the patriarchy for millenia, which means we've been eyeballs-deep in masculine energy. This meant I was going to have some work to do to rewire and retrain my brain to undo all the messages I'd internalized. I'd be sitting at my computer deciding what to post and I'd want to do something fun and aligned with me instead of cookie-cutter. I'd notice a twinge like I was literally being redirected back to the old way by a bossy sheepdog.

That's ok, that's my primitive brain trying to keep me "safe" by doing what most everyone else saw as the "right" way to promote a practice. I just keep talking sweetly back to my brain when it warns me of "danger," and doing my somatic practices to release the discomfort around doing things my way instead of the common way. Repeating the combo of talking to my brain and doing somatics allowed me to change my default pattern and bring more of my feminine qualities to marketing my business in a way that felt aligned with me.

I'm bringing more feminine energy to my work and marketing by:

- Writing social media posts and this book from a mindset and mental space of creativity, intuition, and trust instead of someone else's instructions. Those worked for them and I'm discovering what works for me.
- Being goofy, silly, and having fun between recording podcasts and deciding on email topics.

- Keeping a notebook by my bed and an app on my phone to record ideas, sparks of inspiration, and things that I want to share with my peeps.
- Ask myself questions I'd previously asked "experts" and listen for the answers.
- Trust myself when my gut is guiding me.
- Be open to play, serendipity, magic, and fun to see where they lead.

Look back up at the list of masculine energy traits and get curious if you've been a tad heavy in any of those mindsets. I'll bet a year's worth of pizza, you, like us all, have been operating from that energy. It's not your fault; it's how we've all been socialized.

And if this way of being isn't serving you or feeling good anymore, it's your responsibility to take a kitten step in a slightly different direction. No one person is responsible for undoing countless generations of habits and patterns or for dismantling the patriarchy. Whew that's a major relief!

I invite you to pay attention to your energy over the next few days. If it's heavily skewed to the masculine side, pick one trait from the feminine side and ask your beautiful brain how you can be just one percent more feminine. Keep it simple and just take a kitten step.

You've got this, Sunshine!

CHAPTER 57

Invisible Labor

Long before there was recorded history, there were gender roles. Generally, men are physically stronger so they were hunting to keep their families fed, while women did all the things around the home to support their family. I'm betting this arrangement worked pretty well for all involved, especially when women had their villages to lean on when they needed help or support.

Fast forward millions of years and gender roles are alive and well, and it's gotten worse for women. Men aren't going out to the woods or Sahara desert to kill and drag food back to their villages to feed their families. In fact, *women* are doing the "hunting and gathering" at Costco and Instacart, and way more than the lion's share of the invisible labor in their homes in addition to any work they do outside the home.

Gender roles happened so slowly that we didn't know what was going on until it was completely ingrained into society as a whole. But it hasn't felt good to women for a loooong hot minute. Women have been feeling the imbalance in our souls and bodies and some of us have had it *up to here.*

Social expectations of women include doing all the things for all our people, always being nice and having a smile on our face, ignoring our emotions, not listening to our bodies when they give us messages, and to just be grateful for what they have and not ask for more.

Invisible labor is all the little, but crucial minutiae, that goes into daily life. They're the unspoken, but important tasks, and include:

- Scheduling and remembering everyone's doctors appointments and getting them there.
- Being home so the plumber, HVAC company, electrician, and firewood delivery dude can do their thing.
- Knowing where everyone else's crap is like soccer shoes, keys, sweatshirt they can't find, or last year's tax documents.
- Ordering the dog's special food and allergy medication when it gets low.
- Buying birthday and Christmas gifts and wrapping them.
- Thinking about and making dinner and the next day's lunches for everyone.
- Making sure permission slips and book reports are signed.
- Reaching out to sick parents to make sure they are taken care of.
- Remembering to take snacks to school or practice.
- A bazillion other things that could be a book on their own.

Whether you've heard of invisible labor or not, I know you feel it because studies show that women do an *average* of 16+ extra hours of those kinds of tasks *every week*. That's another part-time job, and that number is an *average* which means some women are doing more.

We mistakenly believe doing it ourselves is easier. It *rarely* is because at the end of the day, *we* pay the price for doing all the things. We feel resentful, exhausted, frustrated, and like we're doing it alone instead of with the other adult we love and married. Our partners can begin to feel like adversaries instead of teammates.

It's. All. Insane.

It all happened so slowly we didn't even realize it. In more recent history men came out of the woods and Sahara and onto farms, and then to factories, and now many are in office jobs. While women still run the house, do most of the work raising the kids, and have almost no help, *and* often have jobs of their own.

Combine this with puritanical and archaic beliefs that women are supposed to submit to and serve their husbands, and our gender is ripe for a complete breakdown and/or rebellion. It's too much for anyone paying attention.

The emotional and physical burdens are wickedly out of balance and our mental and physical health are suffering! It's our responsibility to nudge the pendulum in the other direction and take kitten steps to balance the scales of invisible labor in our individual families if they're off.

This. Is. Changeable.

How do you start to make a shift?

- By being honest with yourself that something's gotta give. You do not need to continue with the status quo if everything in your brain and body is screaming that something needs to change.
- Start an evolving conversation with your partner if you have one. Ask them to just listen, and then tell them the truth.
- Get curious and be a detective. Write down what you're doing. Collect the data.
- Go through that data with your partner and decide together, what could be eliminated and what needs to be delegated to someone else or hired out.
- Remember that you and your family are rewiring your brains. You're changing your patterns and brains don't love that. There will be resistance and that's ok. Keep going, you'll get through it.

This may feel daunting sunshine, I totally hear you.

You only need to take one kitten step at a time.

I'm cheering you on with my pom-poms, Sunshine, because I know you can do this and I've got your back!

CHAPTER 58

Balancing the Division of Labor

Invisible labor is something that can happen in a relationship where one person winds up doing the lion's share of work mentally and emotionally.

If there's an imbalance between partners and it's been talked about and agreed upon, cool, you do you boo and keep on rockin'. More often than not, it's an "agreement" that happens quietly, without discussion, and slowly over time so that neither person realizes what happened until it already happened.

The person doing more visible and invisible work gets to a point and is like, "Wait a damn minute, I'm busting my ass and doing mental gymnastics to keep this ship afloat, while the other person is (hopefully unintentionally) floating along in la-la land enjoying their additional free time and smaller to-do list!"

To quote the Swedish Chef from *The Muppet Show,* "Vert da ferk?!"

Let's all take a sec, and a nice deep breath all the way down to our toes, and a big long exaggerated exhale. Do that a few more times if your body wants you to.

Alrighty then, let's have a little "what's going on in our brains" moment.

The primitive part of our human brains default to seeing things in black and white. They do this because it saves them precious energy they *may* need to fend off a tiger. If our brain can look at something in an all-or-nothing way, it doesn't use time and energy looking at all the options in the middle.

Nothing has gone wrong. We're all wired this way. We just need to be aware of this normal tendency so we can work with it, and around it, or we'll be swinging on a pendulum from one end to the other our whole lives.

I posted on social media about the need for change in the division of labor in many homes. I went on to list three things each partner can do slowly, with kitten steps, to correct their ship's direction before someone jumps ship or makes the other walk the plank.

A Facebook friend commented on my post saying the following, and it was such a brilliant question that I wanted to talk about it. She said, "I feel this so hard, but if we stop holding up the world, who will do it??? Who will take care of the babies and be the change makers?"

Your brain might be asking a similar question like my Facebook friend. I want to tweak it a little so we aren't looking at the problem and possible solutions in an all-or-nothing way because that won't serve us either.

We aren't going to stop holding up the world, taking care of babies, or making change! We will actually have more time and energy to do the things that are important to us individually when we aren't doing all the things for all the people. Holding up the world sounds so exhausting!

Hopefully you're in a partnership with a reasonable human being. One who will listen to how heavy and taxed your body, mind, and spirit have become.

Maybe you're not in that kind of partnership. Maybe you're a single or solo parent. I see you. I don't know your experience, but I honor the struggle and extra, extra work you do.

When someone talks about needing/wanting to have more money at the end of the month, I always suggest they "cut the fat" first. What can you cancel, eliminate, find a substitution for, or not buy more of, because you don't need it?

Same thing goes for our schedules and "obligations." This isn't going to be a walk in the park smelling the flowers. It's going to be challenging and I know you're up for it.

You have to trim the fat and plug the leaks in your life. When you say "yes" to something, you're saying "no" to something else.

What are you saying "yes" to and what are you saying "no" to? This may be one of the most important questions you'll ever ask yourself. The yesses are pretty easy to spot, just look at your calendar. It's a fact that your kids will not die if they aren't in multiple sports each season. You do not have to be a taxi driver, or on all the committees at school or work.

The noes are a little trickier to see. They're usually quieter. Little whispers of wishing you had time to do such-and-such, or didn't have to do "X." They can show up when you think normal things like, "I wish I had time to go do things with friends like my husband does," or "Why am I the one who has to remember to pack all the things for everyone for vacation?"

We've trained our person how to show up in the relationship and sometimes that looks like learned helplessness. That means they're acting like they can't do the thing and you're jumping in to do the thing because it's "easier," which really just perpetuates the cycle that's wearing you out. And you can start feeling like a parent to your person, instead of a partner. It's a total lose-lose situation. It's good for our partners to do hard things and for us to "let" them. It builds their confidence and reinforces the partnership instead of a parent-child relationship.

All of this requires that we change a few steps to the dance we've been having and that will probably be uncomfortable for all involved.

No one will die. Feathers may be ruffled. No one will die.

You are here to thrive, not just survive and take care of all the things.

233

Thinking about talking to your person, friends, other family members, or boss about changes you want to make can make you feel like you want to barf, or come out of your skin. I hear you, I see you, and I absolutely understand. I don't suggest stuff I'm not willing to do myself. So the feeling of wanting to barf and coming out of your skin is from personal experience. Nauseousness is how I know I'm doing something I really need to do, LOL.

If I was coaching the friend who asked the above brilliant question, I'd ask what she specifically meant by "holding up the world, taking care of the babies, and making change." Because we can absolutely still do those things, and for many of us, it's in our DNA. We just believe the lie that we're responsible for all of it or it won't get done.

That's a pretty heavy weight to carry and I'm not suggesting that we stop doing any of those. But when we're doing all the things it doesn't give others the opportunity to help. I'll never forget the time I asked my then boyfriend to help clean out the cat's litter box. He said he would. But I didn't like when he did it, later in the day, where I'd do it first thing in the morning. I kept doing it in the morning because that's when I wanted it done and he said to me one day, "I'll do it but you keep doing it before you give me a chance." I needed to give him the opportunity to do what I asked in his own way and let that be ok. It wasn't easy but I needed to let it go.

A couple balls might get dropped in the beginning and that's ok. You're figuring out a new way. Start very small. You don't have to wash your hands of the world, babies, and making change.

What's one little thing you'd like to loosen your grip on? One little thing you wish wasn't on your calendar or to-do list?

Tiny little kitten steps.

They will give your brain the proof it needs and wants that it will be safe, and others will be safe, when you aren't trying to save everyone and everything. That's not why you're here. To help and love and thrive? Hell yes! To burn yourself out and crawl into bed every night completely fucking exhausted from doing all the things for all the people? Hell no!

There is a lot of middle ground and options between the black and white that's most comfortable for our brains. Start practicing loosening your death grip. It will give you back more energy to do what's really important to you, instead of over-functioning in a way that absolutely does not serve anyone.

If you're open to the possibility that it doesn't have to be all-or-nothing, you'll start to feel better immediately, and can realize you're not alone in this thing called life. Not everyone will step up to the plate, but we've got to give them the chance, give ourselves a damn break, and let some of the minor things fall through the cracks if need be.

CHAPTER 59

Why We Feel the Need to Be Productive

There's a pervasive and toxic belief that I'm on a mission to squash like a mosquito. The belief is that we need to *constantly be productive.* Just thinking about it is exhausting. When you read it on paper, doesn't it sound completely insane and ridiculous? Like who the hell could even keep up? We've *all* bought into this madness and keep at it day after day until someone drops like a sack of potatoes from pushing themselves so much, or one of us comes to our senses and says, "ENOUGH!"

How the hell did we get here? In part, thanks to the Industrial Revolution which started in about 1760. It was imperative for the factory and business owners to do everything in their power to make work and production the number-one priority of those working for them. They wanted money, and as much of it as possible, even if it meant their employees worked in inhumane conditions for ten to 12 plus hours a day. They didn't care about the people, only their own wealth. Employees were scared to lose their jobs and therefore not be able to feed, clothe, and house their families. The only thing the primitive part of our brains are concerned with is survival - work equalled survival.

Before the Industrial Revolution, most family circles stayed very close to home. They were farmers or skilled artisans who met their family's needs on-site. They grew their own vegetables, raised animals to slaughter, or traded their skills with neighboring families to meet their needs. They lived off the land and close to nature. They followed the seasons and worked outside in the sun and elements.

Then the men started to leave to go work in factories which completely changed the family's dynamics. Their time and energy didn't belong to them anymore. They lost the connection to the land, nature, themselves, and I believe we still feel that today. When we're consumed with being productive and getting shit done, we are detached from our inner wisdom, guidance, and crucial connection to nature. We don't need to quit our jobs and become farmers, but we do need to listen to ourselves more when we're getting the hints and twinges that we're moving away from what really feels good and true for us. Sometimes that looks like things just feel off kilter or wonky. That's a sign to pay attention and listen to yourself.

The fear of survival, the puritanical belief that working hard is morally better, plus the fear of being kicked out of our pack for being lazy, and you've got a perfect breeding ground for what we now call the hustle mentality. These beliefs are ingrained in us and have been a part of our culture for generations. To do anything differently feels strange and out-of-balance to our nervous systems.

I can appreciate what the Industrial Revolution did for our society, *and* we're long overdue for the pendulum to balance out. We still feel like we have to hustle, answer our phones and emails at all hours, feel guilty when we stay home because we're sick, and feel really uncomfortable when we even consider slowing down. Our nervous systems have been "trained" to want/ need to operate at a higher level. And it's why it's uncomfortable when we want to slow down a little. The slower pace is different and our brains register that as a problem. It really isn't a problem and we just need to do somatics to tend to our nervous systems and tweak our thoughts.

For generations this go, go, go, mentality has been driven into us since childhood. Some of us were pushed to get good grades, go out for sports, and other activities. Others were responsible for things around the house and other family members. God forbid we rest, nap, daydream, or play past an "acceptable" age. Those activities are considered a waste of time. Why do them? What's the point? What do we get out of them? Because life is supposed to be fun and not a slog. I used to live a fun-starved life and it makes me sad for my younger parts but I'm making up for it in my late 40s!

On top of all that, we weaponize other people's social media feeds. We compare what we do in our one life against what we see happening in dozens, hundreds, or thousands of other lives. Then we berate ourselves because we "should" be doing all the things all the other humans are doing. That standard is completely unrealistic, unattainable, and unnecessary. It's more of the, "If I don't keep up, I'm going to get kicked out of this pack," mentality.

Let's take a collective breath here. Inhale slowly all the way down to your toes…and exhale all the way out.

We are not where our ancestors were and it's imperative that we remind ourselves of this. We won't die if we rest. Are you putting unrealistic expectations on yourself in your parenting, work, spousing, work around the house? Do you have an inner hustler that's scared to slow down? I don't believe we're meant to just survive and slog through life. I believe we're meant to thrive and enjoy it as much as possible in ways that are meaningful to us. It is our choice and decision how to live.

Where would you like to slow down just a smidge? Take a kitten step in that direction. This will rewire your brain and show your nervous system that it's safe to do so.

CHAPTER 60

How to Ask for Help

When I posted on social media about starting the process of writing this book, I received the most generous offers of help from others who've gone through it. Their kindness gave me all the warm and fuzzy feels and I've had a smile in my heart since.

In the past I have been in the camp of ultra independence, which is a response to childhood traumas. Some of the things that ultra independence causes us to think or do are to:

- Never ask for help.
- Not look or be vulnerable by needing something from someone.
- Don't look like you don't know what you're doing.
- Exhaust yourself trying to figure out everything you can *before* asking for help and then only if it's *absolutely necessary.*
- Think that asking for help means you're not good enough or smart enough.
- Believe others will think there's something wrong with you if you ask for help.
- You're behind everyone else on your Facebook or Instagram feeds.
- Your mom did all the things so you should be able to, too.
- People will think less of you if you admit you're not able to do the work of three people.

Continuing to believe that asking for help is bad is going to get you feeling more burnout, resentment, frustration, irritability, and unhappy relationships with yourself and those around you. It makes complete sense how you came to have this belief. Especially if you saw this in your female caregivers growing up.

We can rage against all the systems that got us here; that's important to do for a bit. And then we need to channel that energy into practicing small ways to change it so we're not raging lunatics to ourselves and the people around us 24/7.

It's not our fault that we're here, *and* it's our responsibility to do the work to change this pattern if it's not working for us. No blaming, shaming, or judging because that'll only keep you treading water and stuck in the muck. You get to change your mind about thinking that asking for help is weak. What has that thought gotten you? I'm guessing pretty miserable and feeling like shit.

So what's a human to do then?

- Accept where you're at, with as much compassion as you can muster.
- Become aware that this isn't working anymore, that something needs to change.
- If possible, ask yourself when and why this started for you, so you can notice what activates your not wanting help, and give that part of you some TLC.
- Take little kitten steps in the direction you want to go. Take stock of your emotional and physical load, by making a list of what you do. Don't barf or go postal over the list. You're just collecting data like a scientist or detective.
- Then ask yourself what little thing could you delegate? Start small, nothing huge. Maybe you want a night off from cooking dinner and decide getting takeout is a good option. Or you're on a committee that could use another set of hands so you ask your BFF.

Awareness of where you are, acceptance that you can tweak things, and taking small actions, will begin to create a feeling of safety inside you and make the process feel more doable. You want to stretch your comfort zone, not snap it. Expect to feel uncomfortable. You're changing a dynamic and asking someone to do something they may not be used to doing. It's ok, no one will die.

When you're burnt out, stressed, and someone just ran over your last nerve, it's time to make a change, and you're the one with the power and control to do it. None of us has a knight in shining armor on a horse coming to say, "Holy shit beautiful, you've been doing way too much for way too long. Go to the spa for a week and everything will be different when you get back."

We are our knights!

We are the ones we've been waiting for!

You've got this and I've got your back!

CHAPTER 61

Like Your Reasons

It's common to have a hard time making decisions.

- We don't want to make the "wrong" decision.
- We don't want to hurt anyone's feelings.
- We don't want to make a mistake or look stupid.
- We hem and haw about purchases because we don't want to waste money or deal with our spouse's reaction when another Amazon box arrives.

There's a helpful question you can ask yourself when you're on the fence about anything.

Ask yourself if you like your reasons.

For example, someone at your kids' school asked you to be on a committee.

What would be your reasons for saying "yes?"

Is it because it seems like it would be a fun way to get to know other parents or the event is right up your alley? Do you like these reasons? How does it feel in your body to say "yes" for these reasons? Does it feel light and expansive, or heavy and yucky?

Or are you considering saying "yes" because you don't want to upset the person who asked? Do you like this reason? How does it feel in your body to say "yes" for this reason? Does it feel light and expansive or heavy and yucky?

Feel the difference in your body saying "yes" for the different reasons? Your body is a freaking wealth of information and guidance when you practice asking it for help; pay attention to its responses and messages.

Saying "yes" for the first reason is in alignment with your heart, soul, spirit, or whatever you want to call it. That's why it feels good; this is a great reason to say "yes." Saying "yes" for the second reason would be out of guilt or obligation and that feels like a drag. There are times when we have to take one for the team, but the goal is to do that on rare occasions and not on the regular.

I totally understand that saying "no" can be uncomfortable AF; especially depending on who's doing the asking. Saying "no" to a semi-stranger is easier than saying "no" to someone close to you or an authority figure. This is an opportunity for you to stop throwing yourself under the bus.

You're going to feel some discomfort either way. You're either uncomfortable because you're doing something you don't want to do, or you're feeling uncomfortable because you showed up for yourself in a new way and someone else has thoughts and feelings about it. That's ok, they're allowed to and they won't die.

It feels like crap to throw yourself under the bus over and over; I know from lots of past experience. Living with other humans will always present opportunities for you to choose yourself or them. Choose yourself as often as possible when it feels like the best thing to do!

Asking yourself if you like your reasons can be applied to the hard stuff and the easy stuff. It's a great way to get off the fence of indecision and get moving in the direction you want to go. Start with small decisions. This will allow you to get a little more comfortable each time. It is also how real confidence and self-esteem are built. Slowly, one choice at a time, Sunshine. Kitten steps.

CHAPTER 62

Honor Your Cranky

It's time to honor your cranky!

During a coaching call, a client was sharing how she's been irritated with bullshit at work and she's been feeling cranky about it. She's on a committee that's dealing with a very archaic system that basically needs to be burned to the ground.

When we're cranky about something, that's our inner guidance system, intuition, inner justice system at play trying to get your attention. It's trying to tell you that, "Hey, something's off here, please pay attention and if you don't Imma get louder!"

Start with being aware of when you're cranky about something. It's trying to give you a message.

- Do you secretly feel jealous of a co-worker for a promotion they got? Maybe that's a message from your Self saying it's time to look at why you feel unworthy of asking for a raise.
- Feeling a general irritation since your spouse retired, the kids are home for summer break, or your family adopted a precious new puppy? That could be a sign that you're feeling some grief around a big change and transition.
- Do you want to throw your family's dirty laundry or dishes in the trash instead of dealing with them? The frustration and annoyance is a sign that it's time to talk to your partner or kids about sharing in the workload.
- Dread going to the office because Karen in accounting is going to ask you to take things off her plate and you're so

over it? The dread you feel is a flashing sign that it's time to remind her that you're not her assistant.

Listen to your cranky, talk to your cranky, ask it what it wants you to know, and what it wants you to do. These are important messages from your body, telling you something is off. Don't ignore them because they will only get louder. You will get more cranky, frustrated, and annoyed. If you're still not listening, your body might develop an illness to get your attention.

Then take a kitten step in that direction. You don't have to, and I rarely recommend a 180 degree change, just a kitten step in the direction that your cranky is suggesting. It is an advisor and we've been silencing it for way too long.

It's our job to do this work. Period. Hard stop. Is it fair? Probably not but let's not waste time and energy on the futileness of fairness. You have better, funner things to do with your precious life.

You've got this! Listen to your cranky. Take a tiny step.

I'm cheering you on and doing the same with my own cranky!

CHAPTER 63

Grief Has Many Faces

That feeling you can't quite put your finger on might be grief.

We think we only experience grief when we lose someone or something.

A parent or friend passes away, we have to say goodbye to a furry family member, or we have to sell our childhood home.

Those are 100% grief.

Grief also looks like the transition from kids being in school to kids being at home for a school break. You have a routine you're used to and now that's all wonky. Calendars can look crazy and you can feel spread thin. Notice if you're feeling irritable, annoyed that little or big people, are in your space and taking up more of your time and energy. It's natural to feel that frustration. You love them *and* there's a transition that takes time to adjust to.

When our normal routines are shaken up, our primitive brains don't like it because they like predictable and consistent. Routines are familiar and soothing to them. They don't have to spend precious energy figuring out new stuff, putting out fires, and problem-solving. They could need that energy for fending off tigers, so they send us signals of discomfort to try to get us to go back to the previous and comfortable routines.

We can also experience grief during a usually happy change like retirement. You've done the thing for a certain number of years, with the same people and now that changes. You knew yourself in that role. You identified as that profession and now that part of your identity is changing. That's a big deal.

The birth of a baby can also resemble and feel like grief. As any parent knows, your whole life is turned upside down. Nothing looks the same and everything is different. You can also experience grief when you get married. There are lots of changes happening at once which are discombobulating to our nervous systems. Be aware and be gentle with yourself.

We also feel grief when someone we love changes due to illness, but hasn't passed. When my mom and sister were slowly getting sicker with Huntington's disease, everything about them changed. Their personalities, actions, and abilities. Who I knew them to be, slowly changed. I was losing who they were to me. Our relationships changed. My love for them remained but it was a slow loss, a slow grief. I did grieve at the time, but it's only been after they've both passed that I realize my heavy sadness was from slowly losing them and who they were to me.

The same thing happened when our precious dogs, Gus and Coco, were getting older and having health issues. It was so painful to see them struggle and not be able to run and play like they did when they were puppies and young dogs. Watching their transition was a form of grief. I missed the time when nothing was wrong with them and they were healthy dogs. It hurt my heart to watch the transition.

A lot of us are grieving beliefs that are being challenged. Beliefs like: kids and teachers should be safe at schools, or that we should have the right to make choices that affect our bodies. Some of us are navigating uncomfortable and painful waters as we reexamine faith and belief systems, and lose relationships with family members and social structures.

Our thoughts being challenged is also a form of grief. It shakes us to our core.

If you're experiencing change, transition, a death, or challenges to your beliefs, I see you. I'm right there too. It's hard.

Please remember that the primitive parts of our brains don't like change. It's scary to them because they often don't have a frame of reference for the new things or situations. It translates that newness as a threat and possible danger to your survival and their only job is to keep you alive at all costs.

That's why when we feel out of sorts, it doesn't feel good. Our brains want things to go back to "normal" because they can "predict" normal and that makes our brains, and therefore us, feel safe.

If you are, or might be grieving, consider doing these things:

- Become aware of what you're feeling in your body and what you're thinking.
- One percent more than before, accept that this is where you are and allow it to be there, just for a minute. Acceptance doesn't mean you like it, it means you aren't arguing with reality.
- Be kinder to yourself. Lower your expectations of yourself a lot. Like by 50%. Nothing bad will happen when you do. Pinky promise. Grieving is exhausting. Emotionally and physically. Do not think you're going to be able to continue to do all things. It's a good time to practice delegating tasks.
- Drink more water. Try to grab a nap if you're having a hard time sleeping at night.
- Eat.
- Pee and poop.

This can be your temporary baseline and that's perfectly ok. It's a season, a phase, and will it pass. There will be a new normal. Try to give yourself one percent more grace and compassion. Don't rush it or it'll bite you in the ass.

I see you, I hear you, and I've been in a similar situation.

CHAPTER 64

Getting Back to Working Out Without All the Mind Drama

Someone posed the following question on Reddit that many of us can relate to:

"I started back at the gym [or insert any activity] and went regularly for a few months and then I gradually stopped going. I haven't been back and I'm feeling really down about it. What advice do you have?"

Been there and done that a zillion times with different things.

Part of the reason she's not going is because she made the "not going" mean something bad about herself. Her brain is spending loads of time and energy trying to solve for "what's wrong with me?" and "I feel so bad."

What would get her back to the gym faster than trying to answer the impossible and unhelpful question her brain threw up, is to acknowledge the thoughts. See the thoughts as unhelpful and get back in the gym. Just go. Put on your workout clothes and shoes and go.

But our brains like to complicate everything because that gives them problems to solve. If she didn't see it as a problem that she stopped for a bit, she wouldn't be in the yucky spiral she's in.

Awareness + acceptance + different action = better results. This equation is gold!

She could notice her thoughts + not make them a problem + get her butt to the gym = feeling better mentally and physically.

This is what managing your mind looks like and practicing it has alleviated so much of my suffering. You can apply this equation to any situation. Keep it simple by eliminating the drama, shame, and blame that your brain will want to dump on you to keep you stuck. You don't have to believe all its messages and it's best if you don't.

You got this!

CHAPTER 65

Physiological Sigh

About every five minutes while sleeping we do something called the "physiological sigh." If you have a pet, especially a dog, I know you've heard this but probably didn't know what it was. It's an exasperated sigh that, when our dogs do it, we say, "It's really hard being a black Lab today," because it's a little dramatic.

The physiological sigh is a super simple breathing technique that can stop anxiety and stress in their tracks. It's great for when we, or our kids, are having big emotions that feel overwhelming and uncontrollable. It slows down your heart rate and calms the fight or flight response so you can move into the prefrontal cortex part of your brain to make conscious decisions. I love this technique so much and practice it so often that it's become a normal part of my routine throughout the day. It's like a little break for my nervous system and it just feels really good.

Breathing through your nose if possible, take a breath in, and just before you get to the fullest part of the breath, take a second inhale to really fill your lungs. Then do a long exhale through your mouth. If possible do this ten times but I've found that doing it even once is calming, centering, and relaxing.

That second inhale gets fresh oxygen into the furthest parts of your lungs and eliminates built-up carbon dioxide. We tend to breathe pretty superficially which can leave us feeling tired and lethargic most of the time.

Practicing the physiological sigh feels wonky at first and takes time to get the hang of. Just keep at it. It's one of my favorite things to do while just livin' life. No one will know what you're doing so you can do it anywhere. And the more you practice it, the calmer you'll be overall. It's a simple reset for our alarms, nervous systems, bodies, and brains.

CHAPTER 66

Imposter Syndrome

Imposter syndrome has been described as feeling like a fraud, unqualified, and generally not good enough to do or be something.

If you were socialized as a woman you were taught, in subtle and not-so-subtle ways, to be small, quiet, not trust yourself, not trust your body, sit on the sidelines, don't take up space, and don't hog or want the limelight.

So no fucking wonder we feel like imposters and frauds when we even *think* about speaking up, trusting ourselves, or going for the thing! Why the hell would we dare do any of those when we're punished, in subtle and not-so-subtle ways, when we "step out of line?" Over millions of years our nervous systems have learned that we could be harmed physically, emotionally, or be kicked out of our groups when we do those things.

Enter Imposter Syndrome.

It's a brilliant tool our brains have developed and reinforced to keep us from any negative consequences of our actions. That's why you get that feeling in your stomach or chest, and want to pull back and not take up space. Your brain is saying the safest thing to do to ensure your survival and to not get kicked out of the pack is to not try the new thing. Stay where you are! That is its warning, flare, and red flag.

Today it can feel like our emotional, and therefore physical survival depends on staying in our groups. The brain processes physical and emotional pain on similar neural pathways so we do everything we can to not rock the boat. Our internal alarms are going off and trying to keep us in line.

Start seeing it for what it is and begin to stretch, not snap your nervous system so you can do the things that you feel called to do that light up your soul.

How do you put this into practice? Kitten steps per usual.

- Notice when you have an imposter thought or feeling in your body. It's going to sound like second guessing, a "Who do I think I am?" kind of thought. It may feel like you're going to barf, like there's a knot in your stomach, or weight on your chest. You'll want to immediately take it all back. Don't.
- Do some of the somatic practices in this book to calm yourself and rewire your old default pathways of panic and anxiety.
- When you get that signal from your brain, tell it you appreciate the warning. This will turn the signal's volume down and encourage your brain to put its flare guns away. Then gently tell it you're going to do a tiny experiment to show it you won't die.
- Do the little thing that feels "imposter-y."
- Give yourself a high-five, celebrate the hell out of yourself especially if that feels uncomfortable. This will build your confidence and momentum and help you take the next kitten step to do the thing that calls to your heart, no matter what its size.

You got this! I've got your back!

Outro

I wrote this book for you.

Yep, you Sunshine!

There were things that I wanted to remind you.

Things like:

- There's nothing wrong with you. You have a normal, healthy, and evolved brain, wired for your survival over the last 650 million years. And if there's anything you'd like to tweak, well, that just takes some awareness, acceptance, and kitten steps. I know you can do that!

- You are not alone. We're all walking on this planet with the same human brain, doing very similar things but no one's talking about them so it makes sense that you felt/ feel alone. And if you were pretty much alone as a kid, I see you, I hear you, and I can appreciate that experience. I can promise you this, you are not alone anymore! You have all my words, tools, cheerleading, and excitement for what's next!

- Whatever you experienced and wherever you're at right now, it's not your fault, *and* it is your responsibility to make it better for you. This is the best news because you don't have to wait for *anyone* to do *anything*. This very second, with this book, you can start to tweak the trajectory of your life. You've been wearing the ruby red slippers the whole time, Sunshine!

- I will always have my pom poms ready to cheer you on! Please start celebrating *all* the things you're doing to help yourself no matter their "size!" Hear my voice, see my pom poms flailing in the air every single time. I will always be with you energetically!

- I believe in you! You have a normal brain, you can take kitten steps, and you are here to *thrive* and *not* just survive! That's why you were born and I'm so glad you were!

I appreciate you reading my book! It means a lot to me!

I wish you all the best Sunshine! You've got this! And I've got your back!

Jenn

Acknowledgements

Like everything else in life, this book took a village to come to be.

A *huge* thank you to R.J. Talyor who first planted the seed, that emails I was sending to my clients, could be made into a book. And then for watering the seed with regular encouragement. I appreciate you and your kind words more than I can adequately express R.J.! This book would not be here without you.

I sure hit the jackpot with my developmental editor, Meghan McVicker! From the very beginning I felt heard, seen, and I knew I would get to the finish line with you by my side! Thank you for being you, and believing in me and what I wanted to share with the world!

If you don't already know and follow Simone Seol and Victoria Albina on social media, look them up. Their work spoke to my soul and gave me tools to free myself from things that weighed me down for decades. You two are never far from my mind and heart. Thank you both for the beautiful work you're putting into the world. I'm so grateful our paths crossed!

Jeni B., Natalie Sisto, Jenny Boling, Jamie Fahrner, Jill Davis, and all my friends at Red Key Tavern in Indianapolis, IN. Thank you all for checking in on me and cheering me on during this brutiful book birthing process. I appreciate the hell out of every one of you!

The biggest thank you goes to Sully. For always saying yes to my dreams and wants, for helping me remember that life is for fun and adventures, for helping me heal and grow into the person I know I'm meant to be, and for loving me so hard, just as I am. Being loved by you is an extraordinary gift! Thank you my love, for all of this, and so much more!

About the Author

Jenn is a certified life coach and licensed massage therapist. She lives with her amazing cook of a wife and two goofball black Labs in Indianapolis, IN. She loves to ride her bike, organize all the things, and never says no to pizza.

jennbaron.com

www.ingramcontent.com/pod-product-compliance
Lightning Source LLC
Chambersburg PA
CBHW061143120626
46546CB00005B/1903

* 9 7 8 1 9 6 1 6 2 4 1 1 5 *